'Very moving and well-written, expressive of a moral
vision which is both true in itself and now sorely
neglected…a book that deserves to be widely read.'
Roger Scruton, *New Statesman*

'Raimond Gaita's memoir is a celebration of the undying
spirit of his father…This is the tale of a family's struggle
against the system, but the carefully remembered details
make sure that it is not just another hardship story.'
The Times

'The book is barely put-downable, not just because of
the fluency of its telling and the sparseness of its style, but
because of the tragic story that it tells.'
Salzburger Nachrichten

'Told with impeccable simplicity, with great philosophical
depth and a complete absence of rhetoric…A true
narrative gem.'
ABC Cultural (Barcelona)

'This book is a gift to a man, to his vision of life and
to his internal coherence—a story marked by constant
wonder and the acceptances of life.'
La Realidad (Barcelona)

Also by Raimond Gaita

Good and Evil: An Absolute Conception

Romulus, My Father

*A Common Humanity: Thinking About
Love and Truth and Justice*

The Philosopher's Dog

Why the War Was Wrong (ed.)

Breach of Trust: Truth, Morality and Politics

Gaza: Morality Law and Politics (ed.)

Essays on Muslims and Multiculturalism (ed.)

*Singing for All He's Worth: Essays in Honour of Jacob G.
Rosenberg* (ed. with Alex Skovron and Alex Miller)

Raimond Gaita was born in Germany in 1946. He is a
professorial fellow in the Melbourne Law School and the
Faculty of Arts, University of Melbourne, and professor
emeritus of moral philosophy at King's College, London.

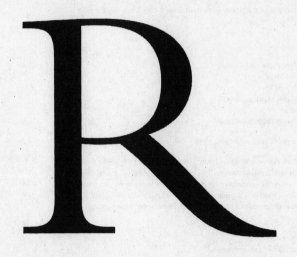

Romulus, My Father

Raimond Gaita

TEXT PUBLISHING

MELBOURNE AUSTRALIA

The Text Publishing Company
Swann House
22 William St
Melbourne Victoria 3000
Australia
www.textpublishing.com.au

First published 1998
Reprinted 1998 (four times)
This edition 1999, reprinted 1999, 2000, 2001, 2002, 2004 (three times), 2005, 2006, 2007 (three times), 2008 (twice), 2009 (twice), 2010, 2011 (twice), 2012

Printed and bound by Griffin Press
Designed by Chong Wengho
Typeset by Midland Typesetters

National Library of Australia
Cataloguing-in-Publication data:

Romulus, my father.

ISBN 978 1 876485 17 7
1. Gaita, Raimond, 1946- . 2. Gaita, Romulus. 3. Gaita
family. 4. Immigrants - Victoria - Biography. 5. Yugoslavs
- Victoria - Biography. I. Gaita, Raimond, 1946- . II.
Title.

304.8940497092

Acknowledgments

When my father died I gave the eulogy at his funeral. Afterwards, I showed it to my friends, Barry Oakley and Robert Manne, to whom I had often spoken about him. They urged me to publish it, which I agreed to do, at first with misgivings, in *Quadrant*, then edited by Robert. The response to its publication persuaded me to try to write a book about my father and especially about our life together at Frogmore, near Baringhup. Barry and Robert encouraged me in this and their appreciative responses to the first draft, together with those of other friends, notably Anne Manne and Christopher Cordner, made me understand better what I was doing.

I am also grateful, for different reasons, to Peter Coghlan, Denis Grundy, Bernard Holiday, Neil Mikkelsen, Susan Moore, Tony Skillen and Konrad Winkler. Margaret Connolly, my agent, was the first stranger to read the manuscript and her enthusiasm for it gave me heart. Michael Heyward, my publisher, gave very helpful advice and thought of the title when all my efforts to do so had failed.

To all these people I am very grateful, but to no one so much as my wife, Yael.

Palm House, Maldon, October 1997

For Katie and Eva

Author's note

To protect their identities, I have changed the names of several of the people in this book.

chapter one

He stood behind the front door of his grandfather's house, with a pitchfork held tightly in both hands, knowing that he would probably kill his uncle if he forced his way into the room. To ensure that he would not do so he jumped through the window just before his uncle broke down the door, and he fled, to return only for a month five years later.

It was the last of many times that his habitually drunken uncle had driven my father to desperate defences. Not long before, in order to protect his grand-father from a beating, my father threatened to shoot his uncle with two revolvers he had just repaired and which were hidden in his overcoat pockets. On the night he fled, he stayed with his mother, with whom he lived only occasionally, and in the morning set out across Yugoslavia to find work. He was thirteen years old.

Born in 1922 in Markovac, a village in a Romanian-speaking part of Yugoslavia, my father, Romulus Gaita, always considered himself a Romanian. His father died when he was an infant. When his mother took another man, he lived sometimes with her but mostly with his grandparents. He knew only poverty, having one pair of shoes each year which he wore in winter, and not much in the way of clothing.

From an early age he worked hard, as did other children, before and after school, helping with the harvest and caring for animals. Meat, sugar, white or brown bread made of good flour were luxuries; sweets or ice-creams were enjoyed once or twice a year. Veg-etables and fruits were freshly available only in season; thereafter they were stored and eaten over the remain-der of the year. Childhood as we now know it, a space apart from the adult world, a life of its own, did not exist in that part of the world at that time. As soon as they were able to, children contributed to the maintenance of their families and to the welfare of the village.

Learning—book and other kinds—came easily to my father. He enjoyed school, finishing his set work quickly and then reading storybooks which he held under his desk. When he was caught doing this, he was often beaten with a stick over his body, head and face—wherever it landed. Bruised though he was by these beatings, his enthusiasm for reading under the desk was undiminished, and all his life he loved to hear and to tell a good story. Many were Bible stories and their memory nourished his deeply religious spirit throughout his life. As did church music. His grandfather had a good voice and sang in the local choir; he also had a fine writing hand in which he slowly wrote church and municipal records. His pious attitude to these tasks instilled in my father an instinctive reverence for the solemnity of church ritual and artefacts, even when he later became suspicious of institutional religion and prone to anti-clericalism.

Primary school lasted only four years after which few children in villages went on to secondary school unless they were sufficiently gifted to win a scholarship. His teacher encouraged my father to sit the scholarship examinations, assuring him of success; an inefficient postal service, however, prevented his application from arriving on time. He cried bitterly, not because of lost employment prospects, but because his love of learning would never be fulfilled.

When he fled from home in 1935, my father made his way to a village about one hundred and fifty kilometres away and there sought out a blacksmith to ask if he would engage him as an apprentice. He was granted a trial period and proved himself more than satisfactory. It is difficult now to believe how hard he worked during his three-year apprenticeship. Work started for him at 1 a.m. and continued with breaks only for meals until approximately 4 p.m. when he had often to tend to his master's animals. He had nothing we now call free time because almost anything he might do after his duties were completed would deny him much needed sleep.

Primitive lodgings came with the apprenticeship, as did poor and sometimes inedible food, cabbage or potato soup, mostly water, or silver beet with sand in it so thick that it formed a mud paste at the bottom of the bowl. To earn money, for my father was not paid throughout the entire apprenticeship, he used the skills he had acquired in his village to weave baskets, make brooms and repair revolvers, the last being the most lucrative. With this money he bought clothes—most importantly, a warm coat for the harsh winters.

My father was not merely skilled, he was a man of practical genius, and during this time his genius flourished because of his joy in having a hammer and steel in his hands. Then he developed the distinctive rhythm of his hammering—tap tap bang, tap tap bang—

although of course the sound was that of a hammer ringing on the anvil. I guess the taps gave him time to assess what to do and to gauge his accuracy. He was able to make almost anything to the most exacting standards, and his work was unsurpassed in quality and speed. Because he worked so fast he was able to indulge his love of reading, not under the desk now, but in the lavatory where he would sometimes read for more than an hour. When his boss complained, my father worked furiously, doing in an afternoon the work it normally took two men a full day to complete. As neither his master nor the other blacksmiths could dispute this proof of his superior workmanship, he was permitted his indulgence.

When my father finished his apprenticeship at the age of seventeen his master implored him to stay, offering his daughter in marriage and the blacksmith shop if he did, but my father was anxious to move on. He went to Germany where he believed he could best further his talents and practise his trade in the most rewarding circumstances.

When war broke out my father was conscripted into an army of foreign workers who lived for the most part in labour camps and whose skills were exploited in factories geared for war production. Sent in 1944 to Dortmund in the industrialised and heavily bombed Ruhr valley, he met and fell in love with my mother,

Christine Anna Dörr. She was only sixteen years old and he was twenty-two.

Slightly shorter than average, she had black hair, a good figure, an open face with intense dark eyes and a musical voice in which she spoke an educated High German. Men found her attractive beyond her physical features because of the way she combined vivacity and intense, haunted sadness. She was well educated and was studying chemistry when she met my father. Fond of the theatre, she read Shakespeare in translation and also liked opera. Despite his love of reading, and feel for church ritual and music, my father cared for none of these and mistook my mother's enjoyment of them for snobbishness, a fault he detested even then, but indulged in her because he loved her.

He had grown into a handsome man. He was dark but not tall, standing at 175 centimetres. A little embarrassed by his dark complexion, he called himself a gipsy and later, in Australia, an Aborigine. His face was as open as his character. Everybody noticed his eyes, almond-shaped, hazel and intense. One was drawn to them straightaway, although they made many people uneasy. He brushed his blue-black hair, which receded from his temples, straight back. His nose was slightly askew, the result of having been broken when a horse kicked him in his early blacksmithing days. As a young man, his features were soft and his mouth sensual. His body was that of blacksmith, hard and muscular. He often sang, with a good crooning voice which could be detected even when he spoke.

At the time my parents met, my father was involved in a minor way in the black market. This enabled him to purchase bread, milk, cigarettes and occasionally clothes, all of which were strictly rationed. I suspect that, as much as anything, this comparative wealth made him acceptable to my mother's very German middle-class parents, who would have looked down on the foreigner with his Slavic features and have been anxious about his romance with their daughter. They had reason to be anxious, for if my mother and father had been discovered together by the Gestapo they would almost certainly have been shot, victims of Nazi racial policy.

Therefore they rendezvoused secretly, often in the cemetery where, my father believed, I was conceived. No doubt the danger and his black marketing activities, his occasional consequent imprisonment and beatings by the Gestapo, made the relationship seem especially exotic to an intense, romantic and rebellious girl of sixteen. During the later war years when Dortmund was devastated by bombing, the intoxication that comes from the violent destruction of the symbols of order and continuity inspired a passionately anarchic way of living which the pressures of responsibility could not touch.

Their relationship was intense and fraught. She was prone to tempestuous jealousy. Years later I overheard my father remind her that he did not marry her because he loved her. Despite the fact that she responded by saying that she knew this, other things he said later contradicted it. At the time, he felt strongly enough to have her name tattooed on his forearm and to try to shoot himself when she left him, early in their relationship. He pointed the gun to the side of his head and pressed the trigger, but the bullet grazed only his cheek bone and part of his nose. Such was the roller-coaster of wild emotion at the time. You could run for your life to a shelter to escape the falling bombs during the night, take a revolver to your head the following day, and the next night run in fear of your life again.

At the end of the war, now married and with a baby, all that changed, especially for my mother. After she gave birth to me, she showed signs of an illness that was to become increasingly severe in the coming decade. She seemed incapable of taking care of me, ignoring my elementary needs of feeding and bathing. My grandmother told the story that just before she gave birth to my mother she dreamed of Jesus who appeared to her bloody and showing the wounds of the crucifixion. When she awoke, she said to her husband, 'This child I am carrying will suffer.' Later she told the story to my mother, and it is hard to believe that it did not affect the way she brought her up. It may account for the haunted intensity of my mother's eyes even at a young age, as though she feared she was doomed.

My mother's neglect of me was more than compensated for by her family. Her sister Maria, although she was almost two years younger than my mother, bathed and often fed me. My grandparents doted on me, joyful in their unexpected gift of a grandchild. I lived with them as much as with my parents. Times were hard, with severe shortages of everything. In the winter of 1946, when I was six months old, people often stayed indoors for there was little food to buy and no fuel to burn. My father would walk up to eighty kilometres for a litre of milk or for a small sack of beans or potatoes. Exhausted by his efforts to get food for us and because he denied himself so that I would have more, he fainted from hunger on more than one occasion. Ersatz coffee became a symbol of that time in Germany, but ersatz liver sausage, made of pulped wood, is a symbol closer to the reality.

Eventually my father found the work he always wanted to do, making fine iron gates, stairways, balustrades, and smaller furniture such as beautiful, beaten-iron ashtrays supporting stylised birds. He looked forward to a rewarding future in postwar Germany, but my mother, restless and now stricken with asthma, looked elsewhere. At first to America, but when she was unable to get there as quickly as she wanted she settled for Australia, where she was told her asthma would improve. My father did not want to go, but the severity of her asthma convinced him that they must find somewhere better for her health.

In 1950, when I was four, they emigrated on an assisted passage on the migrant ship SS *Hersey*. On the eve of their leaving a woman read my father's future in her cards. Throughout his life he was disturbed by her prophecy and often referred to it. She said he was destined for a journey across a large water, that he would lose his wife and suffer greatly.

chapter two

We arrived at Port Melbourne in April 1950 and were immediately transferred to Bonegilla, a migrant reception and clearing camp in north-eastern Victoria. Migrants who came on assisted passages were required to work for two years wherever they were sent, on jobs of the government's choosing. My father was sent to Baringhup in central Victoria to work on the construction of Cairn Curran, a reservoir being built to dam the Loddon River. My mother and I stayed in Bonegilla.

We could not go with him to Cairn Curran because the camp to which he was sent was for immigrant men only. There was an adjacent family camp, but only Australians could live in it.

Baringhup is a village on the Loddon River eleven kilometres from Maldon to the east and twenty-four kilometres from Maryborough to the west. It was the site of large Aboriginal camps as late as the 1860s, and a local historian claims, improbably, that its name is the corruption of an Aboriginal name which means 'river running uphill'. It is surrounded by low, rounded hills rising on the one side to Mount Tarrengower above Maldon, falling on the other side in gentle folds towards the volcanic plains of Moolort, then rising again at Carisbrook, past Maryborough to the Pyrenees. The hills are mostly bare of trees, but covered on the Maldon side by granite boulders, some almost ten metres high, as rounded as the hills on which they lie.

Baringhup lies almost exactly on the divide between the granite country to the east and the volcanic country to the west. The camp was on a small rise which hid the river. It flowed on the other side through plains into a small area surrounded by two hills. This became the main catchment area, the site of the main dam wall. On a hill immediately to the east of the camp is the old Baringhup cemetery, with graves going back to the 1870s, bearing the names of men and women whose families had farmed the land for over a century.

In its heyday in the late 1800s Baringhup boasted a hundred children at the school, a free lending library and many fine bluestone buildings. Its fairs were host to the produce—wines, cheeses, jams and fruits—of many localities near and far. The Baringhup Agricultural Show was a notable show in what was then the colony of Victoria. Baringhup cheeses won many prizes.

By 1950 Baringhup was reduced to a village of approximately ten houses, a school, a Presbyterian church, and the Loddon Hotel, which was a general store and post office converted from the old Cobb & Co hotel where coach travellers rested between Maryborough and Melbourne during the gold rush. The camp swelled the numbers in the school, but there was little for the newcomers to do when they were not working. A large hall housed a market on Saturday afternoon, screened movies on Saturday evening and occasionally hosted dances.

Whenever they could arrange transport, the men of the camp sought out the attractions of Maldon, Maryborough or Castlemaine. Keith Laity and his wife Myra ran a taxi service from Maldon, and befriended many of the immigrants, including my father. Young, pretty and classically Australian though she was, Myra was never afraid of the exuberant young foreigners who filled her taxi and who asked especially for 'the lady chauffeur'. No one looked for trouble. Everyone was joyful that the war and hard times were over.

Though the landscape is one of rare beauty, to a European or English eye it seems desolate, and even after more than forty years my father could not become reconciled to it. He longed for the generous and soft European foliage, but the eucalypts of Baringhup, scraggy except for the noble red gums on the river bank, seemed symbols of deprivation and barrenness. In this he was typical of many of the immigrants whose eyes looked directly to the foliage and always turned away offended. Even the wonderful summer smell of eucalyptus attracted them only because it promised useful oil.

As soon as my father arrived at the camp in May 1950, he asked the man who greeted new arrivals whether there were any other Romanians. He was told there were two brothers, Pantelimon and Dumitru (Mitru) Hora. He sought them out and they quickly became friends.

Pantelimon was twenty-four and Mitru twenty-two. They were well educated, having completed high school in Romania, but they had been denied university study because they refused to join the Communist Party groups which would have entitled them to scholarships. When the communists took power, they quickly installed party members as informers to be on the lookout for anyone who had an independent mind and spirit. Realising what was in store for anyone who valued freedom and justice, Pantelimon decided to escape, urging his brother to join him, before the weight of communism's oppressive apparatus fell upon both of them. They fled to Yugoslavia, were repatriated, imprisoned and fled again, this time successfully. From Yugoslavia they fled to Italy where they lived for a time in refugee camps until they secured a passage to Australia.

Pantelimon, whom my father always referred to as Hora during the course of their lifelong friendship (and as I will from now on), was taller and stronger in character than Mitru and carried him through moments of weakness during their escape. They were both striking-looking men. Hora was particularly handsome. His high forehead, his large eyes and his mouth gave his face an aspect that reminded me in later years of Albert Camus, whereas the considerably shorter Mitru, with his slightly Asiatic eyes, slicked-down black hair and soft voice, reminded me of Peter Lorre.

I called Hora *grosse Danciu* and Mitru *kleine Danciu, Danciu* being a humorous Romanian term for a gipsy. Hora had studied German in Romania so he spoke German with me and Romanian with my father. Mitru knew virtually no German, so he and I managed without language until we were able to converse in a halting English. My father befriended both brothers, but from the beginning his friendship with Hora went deeper.

Perhaps for good reason, or perhaps merely as an expression of their prejudice against 'New Australians' (as immigrants were called), the authorities responsible for assigning jobs at the camp chose not to utilise the many skills of the foreign workers who were almost invariably given menial manual tasks. They were called 'The Balts' by most Australians in the area because so many of them came from the Baltic countries. In the case of my father, this unusually gifted man was set to work with a pick and shovel. He noted how incompetent some of the Australian tradesmen were, especially the welders, but not with resentment or anger, more with incredulous irony. He—and in this he was a typical immigrant of the time—had long come to accept what fate dealt him and felt no resentment or indignation, or any other response which depended on the assumption that he was owed something better. But this resignation did not extinguish his young dreams of a new life and so he saw his two years of bondage as a short interim, reasonably exacted in return for a passage he could never have afforded.

During this time I rarely saw my father. Tensions existed between him and my mother, dating back to Germany, and deepened by her romances with other men on board ship and now also in the camp at Bone-gilla. News of her infidelities travelled to Cairn Curran. More than once my father was told, 'Control your wife, she is stealing our husbands.' When a woman from Bonegilla visited her husband in Cairn Curran, she told my father that I was neglected and running wild. He had no alternative but to bring me to Cairn Curran even though children were not permitted. He pleaded with the camp authorities and reluctantly they allowed me to stay with him, but on condition that it was for no longer than a month.

At the time my father was working on the main wall of the reservoir, a kilometre or so from the camp. Work proceeded day and night. Sometimes my father was assigned to day shift, sometimes to night. He and Hora worked alternate shifts so that one of them could always care for me. At his request, my father was transferred to a job cleaning the lavatories in the camp so that he could be near me.

After a couple of months the authorities at Baringhup reminded him of the condition under which he had been permitted to bring me there. My father pleaded that he had no alternative, no other accommodation and that he could not leave me with my mother. They listened with sympathy, but insisted that this was a camp for men only, that the regulations prohibited children, that they feared that in making an

17

exception for me they had already set a precedent and that, anyhow, the conditions were hardly suitable for a four-year-old child. They urged him to send me to a children's home, but he found that unthinkable. Matters drifted for another month or more.

Sometimes the strain showed. My father was not quick to anger, but when his temper was aroused it could be fierce. Once it flared against me. We shared a room with a man whom I remember only as Schwaba. One day I took a small bottle of his aftershave outside and sprinkled it on the ground to see if it would make anything grow. When Schwaba missed it he accused me without hesitation and without asking me whether I was guilty. My father demanded to know if I had taken the bottle. I said that I had not, no doubt unconvincingly, because he smacked me. I stuck to my denial and, because he believed me to be lying, my father smacked me even harder. Still I refused to confess, and his anger grew till he could barely speak.

Fortunately, Hora arrived. 'That's enough,' he shouted to my father, but my father would not listen. Hora then intervened physically, taking me from my father and onto his knee. I was crying hysterically and Hora waited some time for me to be able to speak between heaving sobs.

Curious to know whether I had taken the aftershave, he asked, 'Raimond, how big was the bottle?'

'Only so small.'

The gap between my fingers measured about five centimetres. I could not believe that the theft of such a small bottle could justify such a huge punishment.

My mother occasionally came to visit, sometimes alone, sometimes with a friend whose husband was also at the camp. We walked in the hills and often swam in the river, me with a gallon tin as a flotation device, sealed with solder, properly shaped and strapped to my back. Photographs show her dressed elegantly. She was now twenty-two and in her swimsuit her figure showed full in beautiful womanhood. My father must have been heartbroken by his unfathomable, troubled, vivacious and unfaithful wife. Pressed again by the camp authorities, he accepted an offer to share a farmhouse, six kilometres west of Baringhup, with a Ukrainian couple and their son who was about my age. My mother agreed to join us there.

chapter three

The farmhouse was called Frogmore. It was situated in one hundred and sixty hectares of sheep-grazing country. Built in the 1860s it had passed through many hands until it was bought after World War II by a returned soldier under the provisions of a soldier-settlement grant. The owner came to suffer severely from diabetes which eventually made him blind and so he was unable to manage his farm. He lived with his wife in Castlemaine, and came every spring with his brothers to shear the sheep.

Only seven and half metres square, the house had two bedrooms, a kitchen and living room. Verandahs ran along three sides and on one side there was a washhouse that doubled as a bathroom until a storm blew it away. On two sides the verandah posts ran down to brick walls a metre or so high, decoratively rendered in cement. The verandah wall at the front carried the name 'Frogmore' in raised cement letters painted green. A small bluestone dairy stood to the side of the house. The rent took twelve shillings from my father's weekly labourer's wage of between six and seven pounds.

There was no electricity and no running water. A single kerosene lamp served us well. The one water tank ran dry in our first summer, and so my father installed a second one. Rats lived under the house and occasionally bit us in bed. Visiting us, Hora woke one night to find a large rat tugging at his elbow trying to make off with a piece of flesh. Long brown snakes came to eat the rats and for a time lived under the house, but they did not threaten us.

The land around was mostly bare of trees although clumps could be seen everywhere in the middle distance. Red gums, ring-barked more than fifty years earlier, stood in a swamp covering a square kilometre to the north. Many varieties of waterbird were attracted to it. A dead red gum stood only a hundred metres from the house and became for my mother a symbol of her desolation. Peppercorns and cypresses surrounded the house on three sides, the fourth being open to the dam behind which was hidden by its banks. Shearing sheds, sheep pens and a milking shed stood on the other side of the dam. The peppercorns, to be found at almost every settlement in the area, were planted as though to mediate between local and European landscapes. The mid-green of their herringbone leaves evoked the colours of colder climates while their gnarled trunks and branches introduced one to the starkly delineated silhouettes of the native landscape.

The stillness, normally enhanced by the rustle of the grass and the sound of insects, was broken when we first moved there by the distant roar of the heavy earth-moving equipment at Cairn Curran, four kilometres away as the crow flies. Half a kilometre to the south west, on the crest of a gentle hill, lay 'Woodlands', Tom Lillie's farm where Tom lived with his wife Mary and her sister, Miss Jane Collard.

My mother came from Bonegilla, as she had promised, to live with my father and me. The Ukrainian family departed within a few months, leaving us their two greyhound-cross dogs, Orloff and Vera. Vera was run over on the main road between Maldon and

Maryborough, a couple of kilometres from the house. Orloff remained to be a wonderful companion to me.

We bought furniture in Maryborough for the kitchen and bedrooms. The bedroom was just wide enough for a double bed for my parents, a single one for me and a dressing-table in between. The living room, slightly larger than the others, was not furnished, then or ever. It doubled for many things, mostly as a storeroom and sometimes as a bathroom, holding a free-standing bath which we brought in from outside and filled with buckets of hot water from a copper which stood where the washhouse had been. Between baths we washed in a deep basin.

All conversation, which meant all living, occurred in the kitchen. The floors were untreated wood, grey from weathering and dirt, and sunk in places. Plank sheets, with no panels or even latches, made the inner doors. The ceilings were of timber, tongued and grooved, as were the inner walls.

Primitive though the house was, it made it possible for my father to keep me rather than to send me to a home, and it offered the hope that our family might be reunited. He was glad to have my mother with us and hoped that she might settle into the responsibilities of being a wife and mother.

It would have been an unrealistic hope in any circumstances but quite naive at Frogmore. A troubled city girl from Central Europe, she could not settle in a dilapidated farmhouse in a landscape that highlighted her isolation. She longed for company. We often went to the camp at Cairn Curran to visit friends, particularly the Horas, and sometimes they came to us. It was then that my mother began her affair with Mitru. I do not know if my father knew, but he must have suspected. She and Mitru were often together, not alone but with another couple, and I would sometimes be with them, walking in the hills or along the river.

A photograph of the period shows Mitru lying under a tree on the river bank with me sitting on his chest, my mother beside us with the demeanour of a young woman with her man and child.

A few months after we moved to Frogmore, before the main wall of the reservoir was finished, the government ran out of money for the project and every-one was laid off. My father found work at Patience & Nicholson (P&N), a tool factory in Maryborough. The Horas were sent to the salt works in Werribee, but after a short time Pantelimon found a job at P&N and some-times lived with us at Frogmore.

Mitru found work in Melbourne in the lost-property office at Spencer Street railway station. My mother joined him soon after, but they lived separately in Dalgety Street, St Kilda, he in a room at number 29 and she at number 5 in a bungalow at the back of a free-standing Victorian terrace which had been converted to a boarding house. I do not know why, but I went to live with my mother in 1951 and she and I lived in the bungalow until I returned to live with my father a year and a half later.

During this period I became close to Mitru and very fond of him. He was gentle, quick to laughter and with a wit that showed the sharpness and delicacy of his intelligence. I did not then, or ever, fully know the degree of his pain. My mother had other lovers and he was tormented by jealousy. Sometimes he fought with them. He came to the bungalow one night, his face bloodied and his shirt and jacket torn. My mother and he quarrelled frequently over her infidelities. Mitru was also deeply troubled by the fact that she did not care properly for me, and that her careless spending undermined his capacity to do so. Unable to afford new sandshoes, he bought me a second-hand pair. 'I could not even buy Raimond new shoes,' he lamented to his brother.

I roamed the streets of St Kilda with a school friend who lived in a boarding house nearby in Jackson Street. We took to petty thieving and begging, for threepence, sixpence and sometimes a shilling. I made efforts to ensure that neither my mother nor Mitru knew about it. Most often we spent the money on sweets or fish and chips, but I also had my eye on a Hopalong Cassidy six-shooter displayed in a window in a milk bar in Fitzroy Street. When I had accumulated enough (I cannot remember if it was one or two pounds) I went to buy it. The shopkeeper, suspicious of where I had obtained my money, grabbed me and called the police, to whom I confessed that I had begged for it. Better that than be thought guilty of stealing.

The police took me to my mother who showed appropriate surprise and indignation. When they went she smacked me, more because she was humiliated than because she was seriously troubled by what I had done. That night she told Mitru who did not reprimand me but spoke sorrowfully of what I might become. Coming so quickly after his humiliation at not being able to buy me new shoes, I think this convinced him that I would be better off with my father.

I returned to Frogmore where, apart from periods at boarding school, I lived with my father for the next ten years.

Soon after moving to Frogmore my father bought a small Bantam motorbike and later a large, heavy Sunbeam, which enabled him to travel more easily to work. As well as working at P&N, he worked on weekends as a farm labourer for Tom Lillie and for the Mikkelsens, one of the oldest farming families in the area, who owned a property four kilometres away. He ploughed Lillie's fields with the tractor till late at night, but mostly he cut hay or helped with baling and stacking it.

One day I was swimming with my mother, Mitru and some of their friends in Lillie's dam. As we were coming home, upon reaching the crest of the hill and looking down at Frogmore, we noticed large black clouds of smoke and a dozen or so fire engines in Lillie's paddock, less than fifty metres from the house. Thirty or so men were standing around the fire engines and when we came closer it became evident that my father was the focus of their hostile attention. He had been cutting hay with his scythe when he saw a snake go under a stook. Without thinking, responding with the instinct of an immigrant unused to the tinder-dry conditions of an Australian summer, he set fire to the stook in order to kill the snake. Within minutes the fire was beyond his control and consumed some twenty hectares of Lillie's property. My father was mortified and humiliated, most deeply so when my mother and Mitru arrived with their friends. The local newspaper ridiculed the New Australian for his folly.

He partially redeemed himself in the eyes of local farmers by his prompt action at an accident that occurred soon after. He was helping Neil Mikkelsen build a haystack. Mikkelsen was high on the ladder thatching the hay while my father passed sheaves to him. He leaned towards my father to take a sheaf when he fell heavily, more than four metres, onto his side. When my father reached him he was bleeding freely from the mouth.

'I fell,' Mikkelsen said quietly. His tone of dismayed resignation made it clear he believed he was finished.

Softly, my father responded. 'Yes,' he said. Nothing more. He also believed that Mikkelsen was dying. It was a natural response to the blood coming from his mouth.

Mikkelsen fell unconscious, so my father poured water over him from a bucket to wake him and then cleared his throat of blood as far as he could. He wrapped him in a lined horse-rug, surrounded him with straw, positioned his head so that he would not drown in his blood and went for help on his motorcycle. Mikkelsen was taken by ambulance to hospital where he recovered. He and others attributed his survival to my father's prompt and sensible action.

My father worked shifts at P&N, unable to avoid it because the foreman threatened to sack him if he did not do so. As a consequence, I spent many nights alone at Frogmore. I was six years old and the nearest house was half a kilometre away. Naturally I was frightened.

Before going to bed I had to go outside to brush my teeth at the tank and, if the moon was out, the dead red gums looked ghostly in its light. It was not hard for a child to imagine all kinds of creatures coming from the swamp, their path to the house lit by the moonlight shining silver on the grass. And when it was windy the house creaked in tones that would excite a fearful imagination in almost anyone. (One windy night, when she was visiting, my mother and I fled the house terrified. We ran down the road only to see a man coming towards us. Shrieking, we ran in the opposite direction until we realised from his shouts that it was Hora coming home from work in Maryborough.)

I took the dogs to bed with me and listened to the radio until I fell asleep. Years later I heard someone speak contemptuously of how Aborigines slept with their dogs for comfort and warmth. I remembered how I had done the same, and was amused at the speaker's stupid contempt. I doubt that I would have coped without the dogs.

My mother came occasionally. When she was there, my father took the opportunity to work overtime when he did not work night shift. He would come home at about 9 p.m. to find that she had not cooked dinner for me. Sometimes he found her just staring into the fire. By the time he had prepared a meal, I was asleep at the table. Only when he recalled this do I remember him speaking bitterly about my mother. She must have suffered depressions, but at the time she appeared to me cheerful and vivacious, even when she lay in bed during the day, as she often did. When not at school, I spent many hours lying in bed with her, reading or talking, despite the fact that she refused to deny herself the pleasure of cleaning my ears with her bobby pins. I was glad of her physical, feminine presence, which comforted me more than food.

Sometimes she was obviously and deeply depressed. Desperately lonely, she was glad of any conversation that came her way, as happened when Neil Mikkelsen came to the house and talked with her. He was one of the few people in the area who liked her, most having taken against her for her neglect of me. I doubt that they knew of her promiscuity, but they noticed how often she went away. My father's devoted care of me contrasted obviously with her neglect and this fuelled the hostility towards her. Mikkelsen, however, was not a man given to judging others and he enjoyed her bright conversation as much as she enjoyed his company.

Forty years later he remembered her vividly, her neat appearance and charming manner and described her as very intelligent and a 'woman of substance', meaning, I think, not merely that she was no scatter-brain, but that she had the arresting presence of someone who experienced the world with a thoughtful intensity. But the occasional conversation with a local farmer or trip to Maldon could not support her in her struggle against her demons.

Late one winter's night I was sitting talking with her as she lay in my bed. My father was in the kitchen. I noticed that her speech became slurred and assumed she was falling asleep. In words that were barely comprehensible she said that she loved me and wanted to say goodbye, that she would fall asleep and then die.

I screamed for my father to come. She told him she had taken an overdose of sleeping tablets. He ran the half kilometre to Tom Lillie's who took my mother to hospital in Maldon where they pumped out the contents of her stomach. Two days later she was released and returned to Frogmore.

The road from Baringhup to Moolort was five hundred metres from Frogmore, connected to the house by a rough track. The taxi that brought my mother from Maldon left her at the junction of the road and the track, probably at her request. I first saw her when she was two hundred metres or so from the house, alone, small, frail, walking with an uncertain gait and distracted air. In that vast landscape with only crude wire fences and a rough track to mark a human impression on it she appeared forsaken. She looked to me as though she had returned from the dead, unsure about the value of the achievement.

She made light of her attempted suicide to me, but

her vivacity was gone. Preoccupied and uncommunicative, she lay in bed most days except for an hour or two when she went for walks. One evening, when she did not return from her walk, my father and I searched the paddocks calling to her, but heard no answer. Again my father ran to Lillie's from where he phoned the police in Maldon. He feared she had killed herself. Later that night I stood knee-deep in the waters of a nearby swamp lit by searchlights as the police, my father, Lillie and others searched for her body. They did not find her and at about 3 a.m. everyone went home.

In the morning she came back to Frogmore, bleeding from a deep triangular cut in one of her shins. She said she had injured herself falling over a log and, dispirited, had spent the night sleeping beside it. She went to bed offering no explanation, then or ever.

Afterwards her behaviour exhibited a strange combination of lethargy and restlessness. Some days she stayed in bed, on others she went to Maldon, sometimes by taxi and sometimes with my father who drove her but did not stay. In Maldon she often visited a Polish couple, Mr and Mrs Smolak, who had come to Australia on the same ship as my parents. To them she complained about my father—that nothing she did satisfied him, not the way she peeled potatoes, not the way she cooked, not the way she did the washing and so on, although the truth is that she hardly did any of these things at all. She and my father were irritable, often angry, with one another. Sometimes she slept in his bed, sometimes in mine.

A few weeks after the night she spent in the paddock, she returned to Melbourne to live again with Mitru. I wrote often to them, as often to Mitru as to my mother. My father wrote only when necessary, addressing my mother, 'Dear Madam,' and signing himself, 'R. Gaita.'

chapter four

When my mother went back to Mitru, my father and I settled into life at Frogmore with four animals, Rusha the cow, Marta the cat, Orloff the dog and, most importantly, Jack the cockatoo.

We bought Jack from a man in Maryborough who, I believe, caught him wild. My father could not bear to cage him so Jack flew free. He slept on the kitchen door which was always left open for him. The outer edge of the door became gnarled and rounded because he used it to climb to his roost. Newspapers were placed at the bottom to collect his droppings. A tin for his food was nailed to the top. Whenever we had coffee or tea, Jack climbed halfway down the door asking for a portion of bread to be dipped into it and given to him.

Mostly he was quiet while inside, but he became excited during Jack Davey's quiz show on the radio. At the beginning of the show and sometimes after commercial breaks, Davey would exclaim, 'Hi Ho everybody!', to which the contestants and audience would respond by shouting, 'Hi Ho Jack!' Whenever this happened, Jack pricked his ears, raised his crest and alternately shrieked and cried, 'Hi Ho Jack!' To amuse himself, he began to pick at the adjacent wall and soon ate his way through it. He did the same with one of the bottom panels in the front door even though it was almost always open for him to come in whenever he wanted.

Marta was a feral cat whom we found in a rabbit burrow. She often sat on the front verandah. Jack liked to strut up to her, size her up, cock his head arrogantly and peck her. When he did this she looked at him with considerable contempt and swiped him across the beak with her paw. She could have had him for breakfast a few times over, but I suppose that his natural arrogance, his visible conviction that their master had placed him at the top of the animal hierarchy, convinced her that though she could put him down a peg or two she had better not go much further.

Marta became pregnant to a wild cat and gave birth to five kittens, one a handsome tom, whom we called Billy. He and Jack accompanied us whenever we went into the paddocks, for rabbits or for wood. Jack would fly and then land on Billy's back, flattening him under the sudden weight. They then tumbled playfully in the grass. Billy was the only cat Jack didn't peck. When they were given milk, the cats would crowd around the bowl. Jack would go to each in turn and bite its ear, until all were gone save Billy. He would then have a sip or two of milk and go off, pleased with himself.

Jack behaved like no other bird I have seen. His loyalty to my father was intense. My father petted him like a cat, turning him on his back and stroking him. Every morning he came to our bedroom. We knew he was on his way quite some time before he arrived. The house had sunk, causing the bedroom door to face downhill, and it tended to swing shut because of its own weight. Jack tried to push it open with his head, but he seldom succeeded the first time. He would get it partly open, try to squeeze through but would then be forced back as it closed on him. It often happened half a dozen times: we heard the slight squeak of the hinges and then the patter-patter of his feet as he beat a retreat. When he succeeded he climbed the bedstead and waited patiently until my father's eyes opened, whereupon he immediately jumped into the bed, and from under the blankets repeatedly put his beak to my father's lips, saying, 'Tsk tsk tsk, tsk tsk tsk.' I assumed it meant, 'I love you.'

As much as any dog, Jack had a clear sense of the hierarchy in the family. He treated me with some condescension, and occasionally bit me just because he felt like it. Even so, he was a joy to me, especially when he accompanied me to school, six kilometres away, flying a little, resting on my handlebars, then flying some more. During the day he flew around the schoolyard, and sometimes more widely in Baringhup, making what mischief he could—chewing up clothes pegs, and other things of that kind—which made me fear that someone would shoot him. After school he flew home with me.

Eventually my father was forced to clip one of his wings because Tom Lillie threatened to shoot him for chewing up his new television antenna. Jack could still fly, but only in circles. Each time he took off with high hopes only to be forced, inexorably, into a circle whose radius was no more than fifty metres.

Still, Jack went to Lillie's. He walked the half kilometre even when my father was not there. On one occasion his heart was set on some flowers which had just bloomed. First he pecked off their heads, and then razed every one of them to ground level. Miss Collard had planted them and, enraged by his provocative vandalism, she was this time ready to shoot him. But when she saw that he could not fly because his wing was cut, she took pity on him and was more than a little impressed by the fact that he had walked from Frogmore. By the time he set off for home it was raining. When he arrived, his full wing was dragging on the ground, soaked and heavy, making him lopsided. He was a truly pitiable sight. Hora lit the fire especially for him and put a chair next to it so that he could perch on it to warm and dry himself.

After some years with us Jack gave us a shock from which we never entirely recovered. He occasionally flew off for periods of up to a week with flocks of cockatoos that came through the area. After one such occasion Jack persisted in going to my father's bed during the day, resistant to any attempts to call him away from it. One day when my father picked him up he found that he was sitting on an egg. Jack was a girl! We were bemused and delighted, but also so shocked that we could never bring ourselves to change his name or even to refer to him by his rightful gender. The egg failed to produce a baby cockatoo.

As well as Jack and Marta there was Orloff, the dog. Like Jack he was a source of joy in my troubled childhood, but unlike Jack he comforted me in my sorrow and gave me a sense of security when I was afraid. Often when I came home from school he met me a kilometre or so from the house, and if I was walking he bounded up and knocked me over.

Orloff was a dog of fine character but without much intelligence. He sometimes slept in the woolshed behind the dam. When we wanted him we whistled. Jack soon got the hang of it and whistled him of his own accord. Orloff would bound towards the house, and Jack would raise his crest and dance on the high chicken-wire fence screeching and mocking this loyal but foolish dog. It happened often, but Orloff never learned.

He was accused of molesting sheep and survived a shooting, but one day we found him dead, bleeding from the mouth only yards from the house. Someone had fed him meat spiked with crushed glass. My father and I cried for him, and for many days I thought my chest would explode with grief.

Rusha was our maverick cow, a blue-roan milking Shorthorn. She persistently broke through fences to run on the road, always doing so when she was about to calve. She gave us fine calves whom we always called 'Bimbo', and sufficient milk for me to drink at least six cups a day at my father's insistence. At every opportunity she kicked over the bucket when we milked her and she yielded each drop resentfully. She chased me around the paddock whenever my father sent me to fetch her. I don't know why he kept sending me, for she clearly had it in for me and, despite her breed, her horns were long and lethal.

One day I was playing with toy cars on the wall of the dam. I must have been concentrating intensely, for when I looked up Rusha was charging me with her head down less than ten metres away. I dived through the fence immediately behind me, leaving some of my shirt and blood on the barbed wire. If the fence had not been so close, she would have killed me.

Those were our animals during most of our stay at Frogmore.

My father decided to start a poultry farm after he and Hora, together with many other men, were laid off from P&N. He bought almost a thousand laying hens and built sheds for them. At first they were unrestricted in their movements, but because they came into the house and shat in it (the door being open so that Jack could get in and out) my father built a chicken-wire fence around the house. With only that restriction, the hens roamed free and drove the snakes away.

We sold our eggs to the Egg Board in Castlemaine. At first we washed them by hand, but since there were literally thousands of them at the end of each fortnight, my father built an egg-washing machine which we stored and operated in the living room. It was a simple machine, approximately three metres long, with a handle that operated two cloth-covered shafts running the length of the machine. Eggs were taken from warm soapy water, cleaned as they turned with one shaft and dried as they turned past towels on the other. Two people were needed to operate the machine efficiently, one to turn the handle and put the eggs onto the machine, the other to take them as they came off the rollers into a wire basket. I was usually assigned to the latter task.

In the winter of 1954 Mitru and my mother came separately to Frogmore, he from Ballarat and she from Melbourne. They had quarrelled and they quarrelled again at Frogmore, with each other and with my father. Mitru decided it would be best for him to leave, so my father took him on the motorbike to Castlemaine station where he could catch a train to Melbourne. Agitated, my father rode at 130 kmh with Mitru complaining all the while that he would prefer to drive than to fly. In Castlemaine, my father went to the market and filled two sugar sacks with groceries and fruit. He slung one over each shoulder and rode home, again at speed. Over and again he asked himself why had it all turned out so? When would he be free of these troubles?

Between Maldon and Baringhup, on a thickly

wooded stretch of road, his heavy Sunbeam developed speed wobble on a corner and became impossible to control. Rather than hit a tree he jumped from the motorbike at 100 kmh, crashing into the undergrowth. When he recovered consciousness he saw that his leg hung limply, held only by the skin, his shin bone protruding through. It was broken in three places. A passer-by took him to hospital in Maldon from where he was transferred by ambulance to Bendigo Base Hospital.

A policeman came from Maldon to tell my mother. She went to Lillie's to ask Tom if he would drive us to Bendigo. He agreed, but only reluctantly, so intense was his dislike of my mother. When we saw my father he was in considerable pain despite doses of morphine, and barely conscious.

My mother was stricken with remorse, realising her part in the state of mind which caused him to speed. The next day, using the telephone at Lillie's, she contacted Mitru who took the next train to Moolort and then walked the six kilometres to Frog-more. He stayed until his brother came, looking after the hens and riding my father's other motorbike to Maryborough for supplies. I was nervous riding with Mitru and entreated him to slow down on the gravel roads. When I rode with my father, no matter how fast he drove, I always urged him to drive faster.

Hora gave up his job in a knitting mill in North Melbourne and came to Frogmore to care for me and to look after the farm. Mitru had gone, but my mother was still there. Hora disliked her and did not respect her. During the three weeks or so that she stayed, his frustration with her grew intense because she did nothing to help care for me. He did everything: made my meals, washed my clothes and prepared my school lunches.

It was a time when I was especially fond of oranges. Hora made sure that I had one to take to school each day. He stored them in the living room, and each day he packed one with my lunch. Soon he noticed that my mother was eating as many as I was and this made him angry. His anger was sharpened by the fact that he too had an intense desire for oranges at that time—perhaps because he had forbidden himself any—but had forgone the pleasure of eating even one. 'Take one or two,' he said to my mother. 'But not so many. Leave them for Raimond.'

It was not easy for Hora to bring those oranges to Frogmore. The Sunbeam was wrecked and the Bantam was broken down. When he got the parts he needed to repair the Bantam from Castlemaine and had them laid out ready to work, Jack flew off with one and dropped it in the paddock where it was impossible to find. So Hora travelled by train to

Maryborough from Moolort station. Each week he carried groceries, fruit and anything else we needed, in a heavy sack on his back from Moolort to Frogmore.

My mother was unmoved by his efforts. When he reprimanded her for eating the oranges he had saved for me she abused him from the bedroom, calling him a dictator and a swine.

Hora was particularly tense and disheartened at the time because a disease had attacked the hens. It caused their legs to weaken to the point where they could not stand and their beaks to twist, the top one in one direction, the bottom in the other, so they could not eat. As soon as a hen weakened, other hens rushed to peck it, often pulling out its entrails through its backside. The sight of hens running around the yard fleeing a merciless flock determined to peck out their innards was a wretched sight. Each day there were fifteen or twenty newly sick hens. Hora could not bear to kill them individually, so he buried them alive in order to prevent the disease from spreading to the entire flock. A few shovels of dirt covered the hens but they moved until the weight of earth made this impossible. The task, and especially the sight of the moving earth, sickened him.

Hora's low spirits over these and other matters heightened his impatience with my mother. The hostility between them created tension between him and me which my mother intentionally aggravated.

'You are a swine,' I told him one day. 'Mummy says you are and Mitru says it too.'

'What does your father say?' he asked.

'He said nothing,' I replied, pleased that it was true, but annoyed that my honesty had denied me the chance to get the better of him. I knew that my father's opinion was the one that mattered to Hora. Later he told my father that if I had said that he had also called him a swine, he would have left immediately for Melbourne.

As is often the case, things came to a head over an incident that was relatively trivial in itself. Both Hora and I particularly enjoyed a chicory coffee-substitute, but before he let me drink it he insisted that I drink a cup of milk, fresh from the cow. Generally I did so willingly, because I liked milk. But on one occasion I resisted. From her bedroom my mother heard me complaining and told Hora to leave me to do as I pleased, berating him with cutting sarcasm.

'Shurrup!' he shouted at her. 'Not one more word. You should be here in the kitchen making your son's breakfast and his sandwiches. Not me.' Hora had had enough. He could barely control himself.

'And who are you to give me orders?' she yelled. 'The Commandant of Camp Frogmore?'

'Listen to me,' he warned, in a tone that left my mother in no doubt about how gravely the situation had deteriorated. 'If you don't leave this house today, I'll take a stick and break all your bones. Leave! Now! Leave me alone with Raimond.'

That afternoon my mother went to Lillie's and Tom drove her to Castlemaine where she caught the train to Melbourne. For a short time she lived alone in South Yarra and then with Mitru in Burnley.

After my mother left, things settled between Hora and me and we resumed our previously affectionate relationship, although it was somewhat changed because, *in loco parentis*, he sometimes found it necessary to smack me. '*Pass auf mein lieber Fritz*' (Watch out my dear Fritz), he warned when I was sailing close to the wind. He worked hard to keep the farm going, cared for me and drove me to school on the motorbike when it rained. With their clay topsoil the roads became so treacherous that this was no small task. Every second weekend we washed eggs, for which he paid me at first a penny and later three-pence per thousand. I saved to buy cement and bricks to build a cubbyhouse. As we lay in bed we talked for hours about how I should build it and with which materials, but after twenty thousand eggs I lost heart and spent my meagre earnings on comics.

Hora and I lived together for three months while

my father was in hospital. When he came home I was happy, but also a little sad. It was the only time I remember when my love for Hora and for my father caused confused emotions in me towards either. Jack, however, was simply elated. He raised his crest, danced and made an endless racket. He kissed my father and lay on his back to be stroked, all this literally for hours. Hora stayed for some weeks and then moved to Maryborough to take a room at an Italian wine bar which the locals called a wine saloon. He often came to visit and lived with us for a time when he was out of work.

My father and I lived contentedly at Frogmore. We seldom quarrelled and when he punished me I usually accepted it as just. But although I did not resent his punishments I feared them, and so I was seldom inclined to admit that I had done wrong. This always made matters worse. He hated lying and believed that only a rigorous truthfulness could give a person the inner unity necessary for strength of character. He was particularly anxious about failings in my character because he feared that I would be like my mother. Like most Europeans he believed the basic elements of character were inherited and he and I were sufficiently different for him to suspect that mine had come from the other side of the family. Sometimes this anxiety made him particularly tender, but at other times it gave an hysterical edge to his anger. It flared when I took Schwaba's aftershave and again when I took a cut-throat razor which he had brought from Germany.

He didn't shave with the razor, but kept it in its box wrapped in tissue paper. The craftsmanship and fine materials that went into its making impressed him and he often showed it to visitors, inviting their admiration for it. When he was in hospital with his broken leg, I took the razor to carve some wood. I hacked away cheerfully until I looked at the blade and noticed that its cutting edge was as serrated as a saw blade. I dared not put it back where I had found it because I knew what I would be in for when my father discovered it.

Anxiously, I threw the razor in the dam.

It was months before my father noticed that it had gone. Fortunately Hora was staying with us when he did. My father searched for the razor but soon suspected that I was responsible for its disappearance. He asked where it was. I said that I didn't know. He asked me again, and then he realised I was lying.

'Raimond, it doesn't matter about the razor. But you must not lie. That is worse than any damage you might do. Even if you burn the house down, you must tell me the truth. If you do there will be no further trouble.' He spoke calmly.

I knew that my father valued truthfulness above most things, and that he would never willingly lie, but I found it hard to believe that if I simply admitted that I had carved wood with his beloved razor I would escape punishment. When he said that I would even escape punishment for burning the house down provided I freely admitted to it, my incredulity put me beyond the reach of his powers of persuasion. So I continued to deny all knowledge of what had happened to the razor.

Three things fed my father's anger: his knowledge that I was lying, his fear for my character and his dismay that he had lost something precious. He smacked me so hard that it actually hurt while he did it, rather than afterwards, despite all the drama and commotion.

Within a couple of minutes, Hora intervened. 'Come now, Gaita. That's enough.'

My father ignored him, but was sufficiently distracted to loosen his grip on my wrist. I broke free and ran from the house into the paddock where I stayed until evening, returning only when my father called repeatedly into the darkness for me to come to dinner. I knew that he would not call me to eat and then smack me—at least not while he could keep his temper—and I trusted Hora to protect me if he lost it. All the next day my father searched for his razor. I roamed the paddocks again, for I knew that he could break into a rage at any moment.

For years he asked me what I did with the razor. I never told him.

By this time conditions at Frogmore had become ever more primitive, but my father and I did not mind. The house had deteriorated. Some of the joists under the floor in the hallway, the kitchen and the bedroom had given way and, in those areas, the floor had sunk below the bottom of the skirting boards. The summers were hot and the house became unbearable, driving us to sleep on a mattress under the verandah. The winters were sharp, with frosts lasting sometimes until ten or eleven o'clock in the morning. The water froze at the tap in the tank, so we filled basins the night before. In the morning, stripped to the waist, we broke the ice and washed ourselves.

We cooked on a one-burner kerosene stove, lighting the wood-fired stove only when it was cold, and even then only occasionally. The cooking was as basic as the facility on which we did it. I cooked breakfast because I rose at 6 a.m. to listen to 'Sunrise Trail', a country and western program to which I often sent requests, and dinner because I could prepare it while my father worked. Our meals were not distinguished for their variety. For breakfast we invariably had two fresh eggs and coffee although I had to drink at least two cups of fresh milk before I was permitted coffee. For dinner we often ate a variation on potato soup— potato soup with meat, with baked beans, with green peas, with sweet corn, and so on. Domestic duties, washing dishes, sweeping the floor and so on, fell to me, as did the tasks of feeding the hens and collecting the eggs.

Now that his broken leg had mended, my father decided he had had enough of poultry farming. He was, after all, a fine blacksmith. Tom Lillie had a blacksmith shop and he allowed my father to use it, charging him only for power, on condition that my father do such blacksmithing jobs as Lillie asked of him—mending gates, ploughs and so on. The black- smith shop was small. One part of it was just large enough to house a tractor which drove an electricity generator, and the other part, used by my father, was not much bigger. It had a forge and anvil, but my father did not often use the forge. He made very little of the classical, hammer-beaten, ironwork in which he took such pride and which he crafted so superbly. Instead he made wrought-iron furniture, fly-wire doors, window screens, coffee tables and such things, which had become fashionable in the fifties and whose steel could be turned cold by hand, in suitable jigs. It was not the work he most wanted to do, but he was very happy to be working at his trade again.

When he first came home from hospital, his leg in plaster, my father was unable to ride the Sunbeam; it was far too heavy. He attached a U-shaped steel mount to the Bantam on which he could rest his leg and, with it stiffly to the front, level with the middle of the wheel, he rode to Castlemaine or to Mary-borough for supplies, returning sometimes with sugar sacks over each shoulder, a sack on the petrol tank and a box or two of fruit tied to the back pillion.

Each week he went into town and bought copious amounts of fruit, often by the caseload. I was unres-tricted in the amount of fruit I was permitted to eat and took full advantage of it. Sometimes my father bought a rainbow cake which I especially enjoyed eating in bed on the weekends while reading my comics.

Our life at Frogmore was spartan, but I never felt that we were poor, although I think we were judged so by others. My father had often told me of his child-hood and that informed my sense of what poverty was. It wasn't merely that we had so much more than he did as a child. More importantly, we were in need of nothing, nor did we forgo anything we desired because it was beyond our means—with the exception, for a considerable time, of a car. Apart from the car, I do not remember asking for something only to be told that we could not afford it. True, I did not ask for much, but then I had no need to. I was always adequately clothed and fed, and rich in what I most enjoyed—fruit. (Later, when I went to boarding school, my father opened an account with a fruit shop from where I bought, each week, almost twice the amount of fruit permitted the other boys.)

Nonetheless, I looked forward to treats at Lillie's. The farm was originally owned by Mrs Lillie and her sister Miss Collard, who inherited it from their father. Its fine stone house was surrounded on all sides by verandahs. It had a large kitchen with a long table and a comforting, big iron stove. Mrs Lillie and Miss Collard often invited me to morning or afternoon tea, always served in teacups on saucers and with cake or scones. Miss Collard made toast for me on a long wire fork placed near an open door of the stove, then served it dripping with butter she had made. She gave me recipes for cakes which I baked on the rare occasions when we lit the stove. At least ten years younger than Mrs Lillie, who was already eighty when I first met her, she did most of the cooking. She also chopped the wood, looked after the hens and collected the eggs.

Stooped and a little shrivelled, she had, none-theless, a very determined walk. Her heavily lined, leathery face showed her strong character and her eyes were bright, signalling her readiness for banter and mischief. But though her mind was sharp she was inclined to be vague. Once Hora came from Mary-borough, calling first at Lillie's house, dressed in slacks and a jacket. He spoke to Miss Collard who greeted him warmly, saying how nice it was to see him after all this time. Hora went to Frogmore, changed into shorts and a singlet and then returned to Lillie's a couple of hours later. Miss Collard greeted him again. 'How nice to see you after all this time.'

At first he thought that she had forgotten that she had seen him only two hours before. He then realised that she took him for a different man on each occasion.

I often accompanied Miss Collard while she did her chores and talked for hours with her. When she went out she always wore an old brown stockman's hat. Jack liked to land on it and, whenever he could get sufficient purchase, take off with it. It was the only time I heard her swear. 'Damn Cocky,' she cursed under her breath. To soothe her anger at Jack, I ran as quickly as I could to retrieve her hat, usually no more than a hundred metres away.

Despite the fact that she disliked swearing, Miss

Collard was not a prude. Once I fell from my bicycle and the handlebar penetrated my leg to a depth of two or three centimetres, high on my inner thigh. When I came home from the Maldon hospital where I was stitched up, Miss Collard asked to see the wound. I showed her.

Her eyes widened and twinkled. 'Ooh Ah!' she said. 'You are very lucky. You nearly lost it. What would you do then?'

Gently she put her hands between my legs to make sure that I had not lost it. Then she poked me and went off laughing.

chapter five

I spent much more time with Miss Collard than with Mrs Lillie, but Mrs Lillie was also kind to me and I was fond of her. Miss Collard went to bed at the same time as her hens. So did Tom who, on one occasion, when the woodpile caught fire around 5.30 on a winter's afternoon, had to be woken to put it out. On some evenings when my father came late from Melbourne, I stayed with Mrs Lillie, who happily sat up with me and chatted. I first heard Elvis Presley singing 'All Shook

Up' on the radio on one such evening and I noticed her bemused tolerance at my enthusiasm for this kind of music.

Mrs Lillie and Miss Collard were naturally kind women, but their kindness to me was coloured by pity, as was the case with most women in the area who felt sorry for me growing up without a mother. My father strictly enforced his belief that I should be polite, especially to my elders, and his success in this encouraged their generosity. He was never short of offers for women to care for me. Almost always he declined them, but he was gratified and proud that they came. His pride was accentuated by his fear that without a woman's love and attention I would grow wild and ill-mannered. His anxieties about this came to a head over an incident that occurred when I was eleven.

I was friendly with a large family, a mother, two daughters and three sons who lived in Baringhup. The mother was an alcoholic, deserted by her husband who was also one. Their house was even smaller than Frogmore and just as derelict. When the girls grew older young men would come from Maldon and it was rumoured that the mother allowed them to sleep with her daughters once the beer started flowing. Originally I played cowboys and other such games with the boys, but later the older daughter awakened my interest in teenage things. Sex, of course, but also, or perhaps together with that, rock and roll. We were sitting on her verandah when the radio played Elvis Presley singing 'Baby Let's Play House'. It excited me and awakened emotions I had never felt before. She talked to me about Presley and gave me magazines with articles about him.

I rode my bike furiously home to Frogmore. My father was in Melbourne and wouldn't be back until the early hours of the morning. I read the magazines, cut out some pictures, pasted them into an exercise book, and wrote a passionate text praising rock and roll in general and Presley in particular, defending him from attack by older generations who feared him as a leading figure in a movement that would overturn their values. I covered the book in brown paper and wrote a provocative title on the cover. I do not remember it exactly but it was something like 'Elvis Presley: Devil or Liberator?' I left the book on the kitchen table and went to bed at around two in the morning. My father read it when he came home. Next morning he was almost as angry as when I took his razor. He tore up the book. How I could have written it? Was this what I was coming to?

I said nothing.

My defence of Presley did not offend my father's sense of respectability as a bourgeois ideal, for he had no such sense. It offended his ideal of the respect owed by children to their elders. His understanding of that ideal, of how properly to behave, was quite untainted by the thought that one should strive for a social status which would enable one to look down on others. He had no wish to prevent me from seeing the girl who gave me the magazines which, together with Presley's music, had fed my minor revolt against the adult world. And had I turned my back on her because her family was destitute and had yielded to the temptations of prostitution he would have been more disappointed in me than he was when he found my book.

Although—or perhaps because—my father had worked so hard as a boy, he asked little of me. Tom Lillie believed I was lazy, and disliked me almost as much as he did my mother, thinking, perhaps, that I was like her. But the truth is that I had virtually no interest in farm life, preferring to read. I liked living in the country and especially liked farm animals, but not in the way farm boys did. Conscious of this and of the fact that I was the only boy in the area who did not kill rabbits even though they were a destructive pest, I took my father's rifle and went to a hill on the far side of Cairn Curran to shoot rabbits for our dinner and for the dog.

I reached the hill in the mid-afternoon. For the first time in my life I was really alive to beauty, receiving a kind of shock from it. I had absorbed my father's attitude to the countryside, especially to its scraggy trees, because he talked so often of the beautiful trees of Europe. But now, for me, the key to the beauty of the native trees lay in the light which so sharply delineated them against a dark blue sky. Possessed of that key, my perception of the landscape changed radically as when one sees the second image in an ambiguous drawing. The scraggy shapes and sparse foliage actually became the foci for my sense of its beauty and everything else fell into place—the primitive hills, the unsealed roads with their surfaces ranging from white through yellow to brown, looking as though they had been especially dusted to match the high, summer-coloured grasses. The landscape seemed to have a special beauty, disguised until I was ready for it; not a low and primitive form for which I had to make allowances, but subtle and refined. It was as though God had taken me to the back of his workshop and shown me something really special.

It was inconceivable to me that I should now shoot a rabbit. The experience transformed my sense of life and the countryside, adding to both a sense of transcendence.

On my return, a kilometre or so from home, I saw a crescent moon sitting directly above Frogmore. The surrounding trees were a dark clump amid the silver-coloured grasses. Even from that distance I could see the light of the kerosene lamp in the kitchen. There were no other signs of human habitation and the sight provoked a surge of affection for my primitive home. I arrived to find my father crazy with worry. He had noticed that the rifle was gone, but had no idea where I went.

Paradoxically, perhaps, this encounter with a transcendent natural beauty drove me deeper into the world of books. My father encouraged me to read. As did Ronald Mottek, the primary-school teacher at Baringhup SS 1687, who lent me books from his library. An eccentric Dutchman, he was a wonderful teacher. He had a habit of punctuating his speech with 'Shh'. When we looked impatiently at the electric clock on the wall, he waved an alarm clock in front of us, and in his loud, clear, tenor voice, shouted, 'Tick. Shh. Tick. Listen. Tick Tick. Each tick and you are a second closer to your grave. Shh.'

The school had only twenty or so pupils at the time and Mottek taught all six grades. (Later, numbers declined to thirteen.) He came to the classroom early each morning to fill the blackboards with work, so that while he was teaching one group the others could get on with the tasks set on the blackboard. I tried to be at school by eight so that I could talk to him while he wrote. Mottek encouraged me to read and to question. 'Now, what would Raimond say?' Mottek would ask the class. They did not know. Nor did Raimond. 'Raimond would ask, "Why?"' he said, mischief in his eyes. He encouraged my father to ensure that I had a good secondary education, but my father was not in need of encouragement. Many of the local farmers were suspicious of Mottek and he was often in trouble with the school council for his unconventional beliefs and behaviour.

Mottek had a deep respect for my father which my father returned. They were, however, strong personalities in ways that tended to clash, and so they did not strike up a close friendship. Mottek also understood my father well and understood particularly his desire—his need—for me to grow up decently. When the film *Blackboard Jungle* came to Maryborough, I happened to see it. Bill Haley sang 'Rock around the Clock' over the opening titles. Quite spontaneously, the youths of Maryborough, nearly all of whom were in the theatre, stamped their feet in time with the beat. I was impressed and excited. When I told Mottek how much I had liked the film, I noticed the interest he took in that fact. He knew that I was attracted to the film's delinquent characters. A few days later, when we were talking before school, he told me, 'Be careful what you do. If you were to do anything bad, if you were to be in trouble with the police, the disappointment would kill your father.'

Most weekends, my father and I went by motorbike to visit friends or to the cinema. We often went to Maldon to see Mr and Mrs Smolak, who had three children, two around my age. For a time we went to the pictures on Saturday night and to church on Sunday in Maldon, after which my father took our washing to Mrs Smolak. He seldom spoke to them of his woes, but once I overheard him say to her, 'My son is everything to me.'

The picture theatre in Maldon was a simple hall with wooden chairs. The projectionist climbed a ladder through the verandah to operate the equipment. When we didn't go to Maldon we went to Maryborough or Castlemaine. I particularly liked going to Maryborough because after the film we always drank a coffee in the milk bar opposite the theatre and, later, because I could play the jukebox. Though Castlemaine with its wide streets and many fine buildings is a more attractive city, at the time Maryborough seemed more lively. Then, as now, Maldon with its hills and old buildings which were preserved because the town could not afford to tear them down and build new ones, was lovely but sleepy, somewhere to take rabbit skins, or to go to the bank, but not to seek the excitement of town life.

We travelled everywhere by motorbike. I was particularly proud of the Sunbeam. It was a fine machine with tyres as thick as those on a small car and driven by a shaft rather than a chain. Although my father rode at speed and often dangerously overloaded it, he was always conscious of how inherently dangerous motorbike travel is.

'They only have two wheels,' he reminded people.

Anxious for my safety, he decided I was more likely to slip off the back pillion than he was to crash and fall onto me, so until I was eight I sat on the petrol tank of whichever motorbike we happened to be using.

He wore a long leather coat, leather gloves, leather helmet and goggles. I wore an army greatcoat which trailed half a metre on the ground, with newspapers protecting my chest against the cold, a leather helmet, mittens and goggles. My father parked his motorbike outside the cinema wherever we were, and I was embarrassed as he dressed me in this outfit in full view of the crowd which gathered on the footpath to talk about the film for some time after it had finished.

My father bought the Sunbeam from Vacek (pronounced Va-tzek) Vilkovikas. Vacek was a Lithuanian whom my father had met in the camp at Cairn Curran. Not long after the camp was dispersed, Vacek began to lose his mind. He lived in the hills outside Maldon, between two granite boulders sealed with corrugated iron, branches and bits of timber. His living space was not much wider than his narrow wooden bunk, which he bolted to one of the boulders so that he could fold it up when he was not using it. Not far from this rude shelter he built a small shed in which he kept awful concoctions that he had cooked, sometimes in his urine. Every so often the police from Maldon would take him to a mental hospital, but he was soon released as he was of no harm to himself or to anyone else Occasionally he travelled to other cities—Melbourne, Brisbane and Adelaide—but would always return, sometimes with hair-raising stories of police brutality towards him.

Vacek often came to visit us and would sleep in the spare bedroom. Invariably he came unannounced, late at night, and rapped at the window. 'Mr Gaita, Master Raimond,' he would call. Had we not known him we would have been frightened because his heavily bearded face looked fearsome at the window, especially in winter, with his collar up and the beanie which he always wore pulled low over his forehead. Sometimes he stayed a night or two, sometimes longer, always leaving as suddenly and with as little ceremony as he came.

He was a gentle man, well educated for the times and of a poetic, dreamy nature. He smoked a pipe, which I thought suited him. One day he bought sausages in Maryborough and left them on the table to attend to something elsewhere. By the time he returned Orloff had eaten them. Vacek had very little money and the sausages were a treat. He called Orloff. 'You must tell me the truth, did you eat my sausages?' Orloff's expression could leave no one in doubt. Vacek then told Orloff how deeply disappointed he was, that the sausages were a treat, that he never dreamed that Orloff would so miserably betray his trust. He entreated him never to do anything like it again. Later he swore to Hora that, overcome with shame, Orloff had promised he would not.

Vacek's sense of communion with animals extended to the smallest creatures. One day Tom Lillie asked him to wash his car. While he was doing it, a grub fell onto the car from a tree, its body arched. Vacek stopped to reflect on what this could mean. His eyes followed the curve of the arch to its open ends and he noticed an unwashed part of the car. He concluded that the grub had fallen just there in order to show him this, thereby saving him from humiliating criticism.

His feelings for human beings were no less open-hearted. He and Hora were walking by the river at Baringhup, beside a paddock filled with Scotch thistles that were tall and green with thick stalks. Vacek remarked that they would make good jam and then ruminated on the possibility of building a factory to make jams from the thistles which grew everywhere in the area. His interest was not in making money. It was philanthropic. He wanted to build a factory devoted to providing humane conditions for its workers.

The summer days were lazy. We wore only shorts and mostly went barefoot. Hora loved the sun and when he stayed with us we luxuriated in it for hours, he smoking and me listening to his stories. He rolled his cigarettes so tightly that they often went out. Relighting them became a ritual whose pleasure for him consisted mostly in his doing it slowly. When I sat on his knee, my impatient wriggling often caused him to burn me accidentally with the ash that fell from his cigarettes. It happened so often that he chuckled at my protests whenever he did it.

When it was too hot to sit in the sun, we swam, sometimes at Cairn Curran and often in the dam less than twenty metres from the back of the house. In the hot summers of the early 1950s we were grateful for the dam. It was not large, only thirty or so metres in diameter, but in the middle the water came over our heads. It had fish and many yabbies that nibbled at our toes as soon as we stood in one spot for more than a minute. I do not recall ever being bitten, but the sensation of them nibbling was unpleasant, so I was very glad when Hora built a jetty-cum-diving-board because I never needed to touch the bottom again. Once or twice, in exceptionally heavy rains, the dam flooded so extravagantly that I found fish and yabbies a kilometre and more into the paddocks.

The construction of the diving-board enabled Hora

to devise a method to teach me to swim. He tied one end of a rope to my waist and the other end to a large pole and then told me to jump off the end of the board. I did and sank, whereupon he pulled me to the surface like a fish on the end of a line. This continued for some days, long enough for me to find it remarkable that one could sink so often before the relatively instinctive movements of a dog-paddle were effectively elicited. Perhaps the fact that I trusted Hora so completely made these unorthodox swimming lessons drag on longer than if he had just pushed me in without a rope to save me. At any rate, the method proved effective and one day I joyfully dog-paddled around the dam instead of sinking. It was important for me to learn to swim, for the usual reasons, and also because Hora was a keen swimmer. He loved the water. When in it, he gave whoops of pleasure, splashed furiously, dived under, swam powerfully, frontwards, backwards and on his side, as though born to it. I needed to swim in order to share this part of his life.

In later years Hora and my father built an aluminium boat which Hora and I often sailed on Cairn Curran. My father and Vacek accompanied us to the water's edge where they swam a little, but they were not at home in the water and were not keen to go in the boat even though it was unsinkable, with outriggers and 20-litre drums at either end.

Vacek sailed in it only once, the day that Hora and I decided to swim the two kilometres across Cairn Curran. Vacek was alarmed, imploring us not to do anything so reckless. When his pleas failed to move us, he insisted on accompanying my father who was to sail alongside us. We were less than halfway across when severe cramp seized my legs and torso and I had to be hauled into the boat. Vacek fussed over me, begging me never to do such a thing again. That night he often muttered to himself how foolish and how lucky Hora and I had been.

My father was made only a little less anxious by our exploits on the water. Late one afternoon Hora and I were becalmed considerably further from our launching spot than we had ever travelled before. With no paddles, we were stuck. When evening came we knew we had no choice but to swim to shore, pulling the boat behind us, and then to walk the five or six kilometres to Frogmore. I shall never forget that night because we had to walk through long paddocks of dry Scotch thistles, some as high as my waist, barefoot and with only our swimming trunks. Until we became numb, only the searchlights sweeping across the reservoir near the main wall distracted us from our pain. When we reached the road we met my father beside himself with anxiety and angry with us both. He had called the police from Maldon. The lights we had seen were searching for us.

Hora often told me stories as we sailed. As I grew older, the stories changed from adventure tales to accounts of the deeds of great men or great humanitarians. Of Albert Schweitzer, who, already a famous theologian and organist, studied medicine in early middle-age and went to Africa to build a hospital in which he cared for those who had not before enjoyed the benefits of Western medicine. Of Ignac Semmelweis, who tried to prove to his arrogantly dismissive peers that they were the cause of rampant childbed fever in maternity wards because they routinely went to their patients after dissecting cadavers without first washing their hands. To prove his theory, Semmelweis deliberately infected himself on a cadaver. He caught the fever, became insane, and jumped to his death from a bridge over the Danube. Hora also told me of a research scientist who was so poor that he could only afford a room so small that he had to open the window to put his elbows through whenever he put on his jacket.

Hora's stories were always of men with ideals, devoted to science or to humanity, and who were persecuted by an arrogant and complacent establishment that cried 'Humbug' when they made great discoveries in science (usually medicine) or philosophy, or when human decency was slowly advanced. Schweitzer was scorned by his fellow Lutheran clerics, Semmelweis by the medical establishment, Bertrand Russell by the political and academic establishment during World War I and later by the Catholics in New York. Like many East Europeans who saw much corruption in the church, Hora was ferociously anticlerical. He spoke, however, with respect and affection for Christianity's ethical vision and for those rare people in whose lives he had seen it practised.

Hora had a strong resonant voice and a fine ear for rhetorical pauses and emphases. He spoke with power and passion, his handsome, expressive face adding to the effect. I owe to Hora the development of my interest in ideas. Inclinations to delinquency ran strong in me at the time. At a certain point in my teenage years, intellectual interests ran stronger than they did. More than anyone else, I owe that and the course of my life to Hora.

When Hora was at Frogmore he and my father often talked into the early hours of the morning, the kitchen filled with cigarette smoke and the smell of *slivovitz*. They talked to each other in Romanian, which I understood reasonably, but could not speak. To me they spoke in German until my teenage years when, to accommodate my foolish embarrassment, they spoke to me in English. Their individuality was inseparable from their talk—it was revealed in it and made by it, by its honesty. I learnt from them the connection between individuality and character and the connection between these and the possibility of 'having something to say', of seeing another person as being fully and distinctively another perspective on the world. Which is to say that I learnt from them the connection between conversation and Otherness.

Hora's openness to the voices of others when they spoke with disciplined honesty from their own experiences showed also in his reading. He read, as few people do, with an openness to the possibility of being radically altered. Many years after our time at Frogmore, he told me how shaken he had been when he read *The Gulag Archipelago* by Alexander Solzhenitsyn. Hora believed himself to be a man with sufficient courage to die rather than betray his principles or other people. Suffering as he did, even though briefly, under communism he had often thought about the matter. Solzhenitsyn taught him that often people betrayed others not because they were cowards, but because they had slowly been corrupted through many compromises, none of which seemed very important in itself. Hora had never before seriously reflected on that. He had believed he would more or less suddenly be confronted with a dramatic decision, and was confident that in such circumstances he would act rightly. But now he did not know how he would act in circumstances such as Solzhenitsyn described. He was shaken for years, unable fully to recover his equilibrium, his understanding of himself seriously altered.

The philosopher Plato said that those who love and seek wisdom are clinging in recollection to things they once saw. On many occasions in my life I have had the need to say, and thankfully have been able to say: I know what a good workman is; I know what an honest man is; I know what friendship is; I know because I remember these things in the person of my father, in the person of his friend Hora, and in the example of their friendship.

chapter six

In the summer of 1954, I went to Melbourne to spend some of my holidays with my mother and Mitru who were together again. My father put me on the train at Moolort and my mother and Mitru were to meet me at Spencer Street station in Melbourne. They did not turn up, however, and after waiting an hour or so I went to the stationmaster who called the police. They were unable to contact my mother and so I was taken to St Kilda police station, where I slept the night.

At first I was anxious, but the police distracted me by allowing me to play with their guns and to put on their caps until I fell asleep. Any boy would have been happy to play with real guns, but I was even more happy to wear their caps. When I lived with my mother in Dalgety Street I was disappointed that Mitru had not been given a peaked cap though he worked at the lost property office at Spencer Street. Often when I went to see him, or for some other reason waited at the station, I asked whoever I saw wearing a peaked cap— railway officials, policemen, once an airman—if they would let me wear theirs for just a few moments. I suspect that I must have asked more than fifty people over time, yet not one allowed me to wear his cap. It is a small thing, but I remember it when I think of the fifties.

I slept the night at the police station and in the morning my mother and Mitru came to collect me. I do not know why they failed to meet the train the previous day. They changed addresses often because my mother quarrelled with the landlord or because they fell in arrears with the rent. Perhaps my father had not kept pace with their changes and the address that I gave the police was out of date.

They rented a small flat in Burnley, in a large Victorian house. My mother fell very ill with severe asthma attacks. I remember seeing her from outside, framed by the open window, sitting up in bed gasping for breath, her chest heaving as she vainly sought relief with the spray she inhaled. The perspective provoked in me a pity that was both intense and disturbingly detached. She also heard voices for which she suffered a course of electric-shock treatment that gave her no relief from the torments of her hallucinations. Mitru had to work and my mother was too ill to care for me. Again she went to hospital, for her asthma and for her psychosis, and I went back to Frogmore.

I carried a letter with me from Mitru to my father, written in Romanian. It contained what Mitru called his 'confession' to my father, although I did not know that. I shall quote some of it to convey the quality of his sensibility.

It has been a long time since we have seen each other, and during this time the situation between us has changed altogether. I don't know how it happened. I haven't discussed the matter until now. I feel that now is the right time for a confession. And the clearer that things become, the better it will be for all of us.

The thing that I want to talk about is a situation whose centre is Christina. A few years ago, a situation emerged between you and her that estranged you from one another, and at the same time this made possible a relationship between me and her. Now our roles have been reversed, with me taking your place as a husband to her. This is the essence of what I want to discuss, and it must sooner or later be clarified.

Perhaps each one of us was aware that the waves were pushing us in different directions, contrary to sound judgment. But we could not help it and could not change course. The only thing we can do now is try to come to an arrangement which will not cause too much disturbance in our lives.

Since she last came to Melbourne, Christina has lived with me. Even if she wanted to, in the situation she finds herself, she could not live alone. In this situation neither she nor I feels good and I think that you would not want this unpleasant situation to drag along as it is now. More than that, she is on the way to becoming a mother. To make it easier for all of us, I want, in this letter, to beg you to agree to give her a divorce. God forgive me, I never thought to find myself in such a situation, but now an accomplished fact stares us in the face. It is preferable not to pretend it didn't happen.

You would be completely justified in hating me, but I know you better than that. For my part, I regarded you as one of my best friends, but in the present situation friendship is not possible. Christina in her turn respects you like no one else. How many times has she repeated this to me? And I know that you are very worried about her.

To give you news about her. I have to tell you that just today I took her to hospital. She had a serious attack of asthma after she brought Raimond here, and became very weak. Although the attack is now nearing its end, she had to go to hospital for about a week to recover, because she didn't eat for about five or six days. On top of that she has been hearing voices for a few weeks now. She had a course of shock treatment, at the hospital here, but it didn't do much good. She wants to go to the mental hospital in Ballarat again, as soon as she is over the asthma attack, and I want to inquire by letter this evening whether they have a place for her there. On top of all these misfortunes, she is very homesick and very uneasy when the boy is not with her. She has very dark and troubling thoughts at the memory of your ruined marriage. If you think it is necessary for us to speak personally, it would be better to meet and to see how we could untangle this, for the good of all of us who are involved.

We have to send Raimond home, and through him I send you this letter. How is your leg? I heard that even so you ride your motorbike. I received £2 from you just today and I thank you very much for it. It couldn't have arrived at a better time.

Mitru and my mother moved to 24 James Street in Ballarat from where Mitru sent a second letter to my father.

The situation with us is as follows. Christina came out of the hospital, but she still has to go there every two weeks, at the insistence of the doctor, so that he can see better the state of her nerves. In the last three of four days she has been feeling very bad again. Besides this, her asthma is also bothering her, not too badly, though it is more or less continuous. When she heard that Raimond was sick with bronchitis she became very worried, and just this morning she wanted to go there and bring him here for about a week, but in the end she was afraid that she would suffer an attack on the way.

What do you think? Could you send Raimond here for about a week or, if he can't leave school, at least for a weekend? This would help her a lot. If you think it is necessary, I will come there to talk with you, but I could not tell you exactly when I would be able to. But anyway it would be soon. The trousers which I bought for Pante cost 29 shillings. I will buy you a pair too if you want, because they have plenty at that shop. How is your leg?

I do not know how my father responded to Mitru's letters. His 'confession' was odd, if not disingenuous, because it had been obvious that he was my mother's lover since they had first lived together in St Kilda. Perhaps they had agreed, and had told my father, that they would separate—and the confession was to tell him that they were together again. Or perhaps it was to record his new status 'as a husband' to her, a status he assumed because he cared for her when she was ill and because she was pregnant with his child.

Mitru's respect for my father is evident in his letter and was evident to me long before. The reason why the two pounds my father sent 'could not have come at a better time' was because he and my mother were threatened with eviction unless they paid their rent arrears. Mitru quarrelled with the landlord who had quarrelled with my mother and abused her. Afterwards he said to me, in my mother's presence, 'Your father would know what to do. He would come with his shoes slap slap slapping, but he would sort things out.' He laughed as he said this. The reference to my father's shoes arose from the fact that, except for one good pair, he cut all his shoes down to the shape of slippers, and wore them like that even in winter. It amused Mitru (and others), and the reference conveyed the thought that though my father was at heart a peasant no one should draw the wrong inferences from that. It was an humiliated acknowledgment of my father's greater strength of character by the man who was living with his wife and had made her pregnant.

My father was very fond of Mitru because he was so evidently a good man, but he did not respect him as much as he did his brother. Mitru was softer and also weaker. My father never blamed him for the affair with my mother. He blamed her (in the sense that he saw her as its primary cause) and, because he saw it as an expression of her promiscuous nature, he pitied Mitru, believing he was caught in something he could not control, which would cause him considerable pain and perhaps consume him. I do not know whether he knew that my mother had already taken other lovers while she was with Mitru, but he must have guessed and, anyhow, he knew that she would, sooner rather than later. 'She was a woman who liked men,' my father was to say later. He did not say this angrily. His tone was sorrowful and resigned.

My father did not agree to a divorce because, as he put it, he did not 'believe in divorce'. Whatever his feelings were about Mitru's confession, and towards my mother, he allowed her to stay with us for a month or so from early May in 1955. From Frogmore she wrote a letter to Maria, her sister in Germany, telling her that she was pregnant, but she wrote suggesting, without saying so explicitly, that it was my father's child and that we were again a family.

Perhaps she and my father had discussed the chances of a reconciliation, because for the time she was there she tried harder than I ever remember to care for me and the house. She made curtains for the windows, cleaned and occasionally cooked. On my ninth birthday we lit the stove and she cooked a *Sauerbraten* (a traditional German beef dish) for us and for the family of a school friend who came to celebrate with us. She burnt the meat, but so rare was the experience of her preparing any kind of meal that I have since had a fondness for burnt meat.

Again, I remember her as cheerful and lively, even

when she had hallucinations. One day she was washing clothes in a basin in the kitchen. An operatic aria was playing on the radio and she sang with it, telling me about opera and how much she enjoyed it. Suddenly she asked, 'Do you hear those voices?'

'You mean the voices on the radio?'

'No, the other voices. Can't you hear them? Up there,' she said, pointing upwards, but beyond that to nowhere in particular.

Alarmed, I ran outside, right around the house. I even climbed onto the roof to see if there was anyone there, hoping to find someone, ominous though that would have been, rather than accept that my mother was mad. Of course there was no one.

After that she no longer asked me if I heard anything, but sometimes told me when she did. To my deep disappointment she left us to live again with Mitru, this time in Maryborough. Less than two months later, she gave birth to a baby girl, Susan.

My mother and Mitru rented a room at the back of the wine saloon in Maryborough. The owners, Mr and Mrs Foschia, had long been friends of my father, and Hora had also stayed there at times. They had a son, Dominic, who was kind to me although he was some years older. I often visited my mother and Mitru there and sometimes stayed for weekends, in a separate room paid for by my father.

The saloon itself occupied a smallish room at the front of one of the more imposing Victorian buildings in High Street. In a much larger room across the passage Mr Foschia kept his barrels. The saloon's customers were predominantly immigrants who lived in the area, but it was also home to a small group of mostly Australian alcoholics. Mr Foschia—known to everyone as Gino—kept an insecure order in the bar and the fragility of this achievement made him tense. Every hour or so he came to the back of the house, walking with a heavy step, scraping his boots on the stone floor of the verandah, swearing in Italian. '*Ostia! Porco Dio! Porca Madonna!*' he shouted in a gravelly voice. He then spat into the gully-trap, turned on the tap to wash the spit away and returned to the bar. After he had closed the saloon around 5 p.m., he relaxed by standing in his front doorway, his thumbs in his braces, surveying events in the street and greeting passers-by.

Despite Mr Foschia's roughness I was fond of him and never frightened by him. His wife was a different and more formidable proposition. A small, plump woman, grey-haired and with a sharp tongue, she kept a firmer, more mercenary, hand on things than her soft-hearted husband. She prepared meals for lodgers in an enormous dining room and did their washing, but she also kept an eye on her husband at the bar to ensure that he did not yield to the temptation occasionally to give the chronic alcoholics free drinks. Her disapproval of my mother was never far from the surface. She made no effort to hide it from me which made me dislike her and feel uneasy in her company. My father complained of her financial meanness, but thought her to be a good, hard-working and upright woman, whose strengths saved her husband from ruin.

Mrs Foschia ruled the entire house, but her stern presence was felt especially at the back where my mother and Mitru lived in a small room which barely held a double bed, a dresser and a wardrobe. They cooked and showered in separate, communal facilities. Their room faced the backyard which was almost bare of vegetation, and was intolerably hot in summer despite being protected from direct sunlight by the verandah. My mother and Mitru often sat under the verandah and Susan often lay there in her pram. Mercifully, the botanical gardens were on the other side of the back street. There they could lie on the cool grass under the shade of one of the many fine trees.

Not long after Susan was born, my mother again fell into the pattern of neglect that had begun with my birth. She lay in bed, read magazines, walked around the town, but would not change Susan's nappies even when Susan developed nappy rash and cried in pain. Mitru worked at the wire works and rushed home at lunch time to change Susan's nappies. He said that he could barely wait for the siren to sound, so anxious was he to go home to attend to her.

My mother and he quarrelled, over Susan, and over the fact that rent was again in arrears because my mother would sometimes spend his wages of approximately eight pounds per week on dresses costing twenty or thirty pounds. Mitru took a second job, running home whenever he could during breaks in order to care for Susan. His misery was compounded by the fact that my mother flirted with some young men who boarded in the same building. They whistled at her, and told her she had beautiful legs. 'And so I have,' she said to me, flattered by their attentions.

Mrs Foschia complained to my father about the quarrelling and the fact that the rent was so far behind. He paid the arrears and some in advance but, when he told Mitru that the Foschias' patience was at an end, they argued. Mitru hit my father. Although my father was much stronger than Mitru, he did not return the blow. Mitru cried and apologised. He said he could stand my mother no longer, that he was 'at the end'. My father suggested he leave and send her money. If he could not afford that, my father would help out. Mitru refused both to leave my mother and the offer of help.

Relations between Mitru and my mother became

ever more desperate. Early in November, he rode his bicycle into the bush outside Maryborough and stabbed himself in the chest, just below the heart. He was found, unconscious, by a passer-by who took him to hospital where he stayed a few days. In hospital he was visited by the local police sergeant because suicide was then a criminal offence. He was not charged, but the policeman demanded that Mitru undertake never to do it again. Mitru refused.

He refused the policeman, but he did not refuse my mother. Responding to her pleas, he promised that he would not try to kill himself again. But the drama of his attempted suicide, and the anxious and tender emotions it released, did not change things between them for long. Mitru recovered only to find himself in the same situation from which he had sought release. Soon they quarrelled again, as bitterly as before, and my mother went to stay with Susan's godparents, an Italian couple who lived less than a kilometre away.

One weekend when I was staying with my mother at the home of Susan's godparents, my father brought Hora there. He knew of his brother's misery and it pained him. He wanted to see him, to speak to him in the hope that he could help and comfort him. But, once there, irritated by the presence of my mother and distraught at the sight of how abject Mitru had become,

Hora's distress became mixed with anger and he harshly broke the silence he had kept to that day about Mitru's relationship with my mother.

'How can you let yourself fall so low?' he demanded of Mitru. 'How can you let yourself be trampled down by such a characterless woman? Why don't you wake up and see what you have done to yourself?' Hora did not ask these questions rhetorically but, even more than wanting an answer for himself, he wanted Mitru seriously to put them to himself.

Mitru couldn't bear it. 'You'd better go,' he said, 'and don't come to see me again.'

'All right, I'll go,' Hora replied. 'You can come and see me if you want, but if you come, come by yourself— not with her.' He pointed to my mother.

Remorse beset him even before he was out of the door and all his life he regretted saying 'but not with her'.

A fortnight later on a hot day, early in the summer of 1956, a friend drove Mitru to Frogmore. Hora had come from Melbourne and Mitru knew it, for my father had told him. He came hoping they could be reconciled. The four men drank and talked happily. Neither Hora nor Mitru mentioned their quarrel, but it was clear that both wanted to put it behind them. Mitru had brought Susan with him and, at my father's suggestion, she lay without a nappy, under the verandah in the cool and drying breeze.

'Look how beautiful she is,' my father said.

'Yes, she is beautiful,' Mitru replied. 'What a pity she receives no attention from her mother. If it were not for me, who knows what state she would be in.'

A few weeks later, I stayed with my mother and Mitru who were again living together at the back of the wine saloon. The summer was hot and often debilitating. Red-raw with nappy rash, Susan cried a lot. I wheeled her in her pram for hours to get her away from my mother who could not bear her crying. As so often before, she lay in bed reading magazines and listening to the radio. She quarrelled with Mrs Foschia who reprimanded her for not caring for her baby.

'I could perhaps stand it, if only Christina was quiet,' Mitru had told his brother. Instead, she lacerated him with a caustic tongue. One evening he beat her with his belt. It was a measure of my affection for him, and my sense of his desperation, that I did not resent him for beating my mother, even though I saw him do it and even though she complained bitterly to me, showing her many bruises.

They made up the next day. I remember him stripped to the waist, and her affectionately tending the wounds he inflicted on himself when he tried to commit suicide. It was a balmy night, the sky clear and tending to purple. Relieved at the sight of their affection for one another, I went to the cinema which was screening *The Garden of Evil*, starring Gary Cooper and Rita Hayworth. My mother was a Hayworth fan. Even as a boy of nine, I could see why. Hayworth's sensual eroticism was of the kind my father had noted when he said of my mother 'she liked men'.

A week later Mitru came home from work at midday and fought with my mother over her neglect of Susan. He beat her again with his belt, bruising her about the arms and body with its buckle. Susan lay in her pram on the verandah, crying. Mitru took her in his arms and went off with her, but came back within an hour. He then rode his bicycle to the Pioneers' Memorial Tower and dived fifteen metres to his death. My mother was three months pregnant.

I learned that Mitru was dead when my mother arrived at my school in a taxi at approximately three o'clock the next Monday afternoon. My father was with her. She was in the back seat, her head covered with a light scarf, her face drawn and marked with tears. She told me that Mitru had died and, when I asked how, she said that he had died of a cold. That evening she told me the truth, and that she had spent the previous two nights sleeping at the foot of the tower, fighting the impulse to follow him. She said that he was so determined to succeed this time that he placed a knife at the foot of the tower onto which he intended to fall. I do not know whether this horrible detail is true.

That night she stayed at Frogmore, and the next day my father took her to Susan's godparents in Maryborough. My father arranged the funeral. The Catholic priest refused to bury Mitru because he had committed suicide. My father then went to the Anglican priest. 'Will you bury this man, even though he killed himself?'

'Of course,' the priest replied. 'He's not a dog, he's a human being.'

Mourners, many of whom were friends of both brothers and of my mother, came from Melbourne. Mitru lay in an open coffin, his face broken and dark purple with bruising. People took photographs, close up, almost next to his face. The memory of it haunted me for years. My mother came to the graveside with her friends and stood separately, weeping bitterly. After the funeral, mourners gathered for drinks at the Foschias'. I remember Hora at a distance from the gathering, his face twisted in grief and with what I read as despair.

No one knows why Mitru killed himself. There can be no doubt that the strain of living with my mother was the main reason for his desperate state of mind. At the inquest my mother testified that when she suggested that it might be better for them to part than to quarrel so bitterly, he replied that he could not live without her and the baby, and that if she left he would kill himself. My father believed that Mitru felt humiliated by the fact that my father had paid his and my mother's rent, and even more because my father did not strike back when Mitru hit him. Hora believed Mitru feared that one day out of anger and frustration he would beat my mother again and that, goaded further by her taunts, would actually kill her. Rather than have her death and the death of the child she was carrying on his conscience, he killed himself. Mitru believed in an afterlife and a last judgment, but he believed that the judgment you passed was on yourself, that it was inescapable because it was intrinsic to your acknowledgment of your guilt, and that you were eternally answerable to it.

Very likely my mother, my father and Hora were all partly right. In his own eyes Mitru was a wretched man. He had taken the wife of a friend before whom he felt guilty and humiliated. His wrongdoing was unredeemed, for it brought happiness to no one and much misery. I do not know how often he beat my mother, but I know that he would have been mortified and frightened by his capacity for such violence. He could not leave her; he loved her too much. It is likely that he felt that it was better to die than to compound the guilt, the shame and the misery with murder. He was twenty-seven. A stone cross marks his grave. It carries the epitaph, CREDINTA IN ZELELE DE APOI/E SINGURA NADEJDE IN NOI (Belief in the afterlife is the only hope in us).

chapter seven

For some time after Mitru's death my father was distant and preoccupied, brooding on his and my mother's parts in it. I felt his absence and once, when he smacked me, I shouted from the bedroom to where I had retreated, 'You don't love me.'

He came to the door and stood there, very serious, looking at me for some time. 'Do you believe that? Do you really?' he asked.

I shrugged, turned away from him and said, 'Yes.'

I didn't believe it, but I told him that I did because I had registered the effect of my accusation on him and I wanted to make the most of it. He went away obviously troubled.

I thought nothing more of it until that weekend when I had reason to regret my words bitterly. We were in Maryborough intending to go to the pictures. As was often the case, we went late in the afternoon so that my father could first visit friends. Whenever I could, I avoided these visits because I found them boring, especially as the conversation would be in Romanian, Yugoslav, Polish or Italian. I wandered about Maryborough and sometimes went to the Foschias for dinner. My father and I would meet at the cinema after the film. He seldom came until the second feature, and sometimes not until the end.

I was at the Foschias on this occasion when the telephone rang around six. Mr Foschia called me to the phone. It was the Maryborough hospital. My father had been in an accident. His motorbike had collided with a car. Could I come straightaway?

When I arrived at the hospital I had to wait for over half an hour. I heard loud moaning and gurgling in someone's throat and chest as though they were drowning in their blood. I prayed it was not my father. When a nurse took me to see him, I knew the sounds came from him. He had severe head injuries. His face was bruised and covered in dried blood and his nose was broken. I remembered Mitru in his coffin. A tube in my father's mouth had been responsible for the sounds I had heard. He tried a number of times to speak and eventually succeeded, each word causing him severe pain. 'Never believe that I don't love you.' That was all he said to me that evening.

After a month or so when he recovered physically, his work brought my father again into spiritual equilibrium. Never willingly an early riser, he went to Tom Lillie's blacksmith shop at nine, and then worked late into the night, until ten or eleven, and on most weekends. He would occasionally watch an hour or so of television when the Lillies bought a set, but he was happiest in his workshop, spending little time at Frogmore. He played Romanian and Yugoslav records on a record player in the middle of the workshop, singing along with them. He was fond of crooners, particularly of Dean Martin for his easygoing style, but he admired Bing Crosby more for his capacity suddenly to hit a low note.

I have never seen a workman as skilled as my father. His unboastful confidence in what he could do impressed me as much as his achievements. He was so at ease with his materials and always so respectful of their nature that they seemed in friendship with him, as though consenting to his touch rather than subjugated by him.

This extended beyond his ironwork. He made the jeans we wore and for both of us good, 'Sunday' trousers. He mended and made shoes. As an expression of gratitude to a woman who had been kind to him he made a beautiful lace curtain, the lace included. From old sheep bones he found in the paddocks he made cigarette holders and handles for the knives he also made. He carved wood and later in his life made himself a lathe on which he crafted a fine spinning wheel with which he spun wool.

He repaired almost everything: motorbikes, cars, welders and clocks, often making the tools and parts, including the clockwork parts, himself. He was a superb welder and his reputation spread among the farmers in the region. When they brought him something to weld he said, 'If this breaks, it will not break where I weld. It will break somewhere else.' Invariably he was right. In those days he welded only with oxyacetylene, using a piece of baling wire.

His work both expressed and formed much of his character. From him I learned the relation between work and character. His sense of the importance of work and of its moral and spiritual requirements was simple and noble. Like him, his work was honest through and through. He worked at great speed, able to cut steel by sight to within a millimetre, yet everything was perfectly made. If there was a fault, as sometimes occurred because of the qualities of his material, or because, as happened later, one of his workmen was careless, he took immediate and full responsibility. He accepted responsibility because he believed that it was the duty of an honest person to do so. It was inconceivable to him that he should do so, because, for example, it would rebound on him if he did not—as inconceivable as that he should be truthful for similar reasons. He regarded such prudential justifications— that honesty pays, for example—as shabby. The refusal of such justifications was for him and for Hora the mark of our humanity.

Gradually his reputation as a workman spread to neighbouring towns. Friendly shopkeepers allowed him to display his work in their windows and he exhibited in local shows in Maldon, Maryborough, Castlemaine, Bendigo and Ballarat. Through such publicity and by word of mouth his work became admired and his business prospered.

He was deeply gratified that his work, and he through it, should become respected. Many times he told me that there are few things more important than a good name. Again, his reasons were not prudential. He took pleasure only in the esteem of those whom he knew to be deserving to judge him and his work. The praise of the lazy, the dishonest or those whose character and work were shoddy meant nothing to him.

In this respect he belonged to a long tradition of European thought which celebrated, as an essential constituent of a fulfilled human life, a community of equals, each worthy to rejoice in the virtues and achievements of the other.

My father would have taken pleasure in his good name anywhere, but he had an additional reason for it in Baringhup. Those were the days before multi-culturalism—immigrants were tolerated, but seldom accorded the respect they deserved. It occurred to few of the men and women of central Victoria that the foreigners in their midst might live their lives and judge their surroundings in the light of standards which were equal and sometimes superior to theirs. That is why it never seriously occurred to them to call my father by his name, Romulus. They called him Jack.

Both Hora and my father were appreciative of the tolerance shown to them by Australians, and both knew it to be greater than could be expected in most European nations. Hora felt this especially strongly because he had rebelled against communist rule in Romania and suffered for it. For a long time he found it hard fully to believe that there could exist such freedom and tolerance as he found in Australia. He sometimes expressed this in comical ways. When Jack the cockatoo shat in the house or in other ways indulged his inclination to assert ownership of it, Hora laughed and exclaimed, 'That's right. That how it is. It's *Demo-kra-cy*!' Nonetheless, for proud men such as they were, the condescension of their neighbours must have rankled.

They were not proud in any sense that implies arrogance, and certainly not in any sense that implies they wanted respect for reasons other than their serious attempt to live decently. I have never known anyone who lived so passionately, as did these two friends, the belief that nothing matters so much in life as to live it decently. Nor have I known anyone so resistant and contemptuous, throughout their lives, of the external signs of status and prestige. They recognised this in each other, and it formed the basis of their deep and life-long friendship. But I know from their disappointments that they longed for a community of honourable men and women who humbly, but without humbug, knew their own worth and the worth of others.

Character—or *karacter* as they pronounced it, with the emphasis on the second syllable—was the central moral concept for my father and Hora. It stood for a settled disposition for which it was possible rightly to admire someone. The men and women in Baringhup and its surroundings in the fifties respected character, even when, rarely, they had little of it themselves. Honesty, loyalty, courage, charity (taken as a preparedness to help others in need) and a capacity for hard work were the virtues most prized by the men and women I knew then.

In their words and actions they expressed a suspicion of *personality* because they believed it to be superficial and changeable. Theirs was a puritanical conception of human possibilities, but its tendency to be dour was relieved by an idea that belonged to the same stable as that of character. It was the notion of *a character* and, like its parent, it suggested something steady and deep in a person. It was possible to be a character while living a hermit's life in the bush, but one could not be a personality that way. They thought a dazzling personality was merely the false semblance of real individuality as it displayed itself in the person who had become a character.

Tom Lillie and others disliked my mother partly because they saw her engaging vivacity as a dangerously seductive manifestation of personality in a woman they believed to be lacking entirely in character—a 'characterless woman' as Hora put it. Miss Collard, by comparison, had character and was a character. Mrs Lillie had character but was less of a character than her sister because of her desire to be 'proper', a 'respectable' wife to a man with a distinguished name in the farming community. Perhaps that is why I once surprised Tom with Miss Collard on his knee.

Such was the division of the human spirit in that

part of the world at that time. Like other sharp divisions, it could not capture the many worthy ways of being human. It nourished some possibilities, maimed others and would not allow some even to see the light of day. Women particularly suffered under it. Its tendency to puritanism was probably ineradicable, closing off the perspective from which men could unreservedly glory in feminine beauty and grace. It offered to women ideals of femininity cut off from sensuality, and so, paradoxically, offered them an ideal of femininity that undermined their potential truly to be women.

Perhaps that is why women at that time and in that place were especially vulnerable to the deadening attractions of middle-class respectability. Foreign women, with historically deeper and more complex traditions of womanhood still alive in them, tended to manage better. They were also attracted to wealth more for reasons connected with status than with greed, but for many of the East Europeans a tendency to vulgarity countered any inclination they had to turn the achievement of status into an ersatz morality.

But for someone like my mother, highly intelligent, deeply sensuous, anarchic and unstable, this emphasis on character, given an Australian accent, provided the wrong conceptual environment for her to find herself and for others to understand her. Tom Lillie's contempt for her was common. It was also emblematic of a culture whose limitations were partly the reason she could not overcome hers.

One Anzac Day I heard on the radio a poem written by an English poet during World War II. It was a hymn of praise to the qualities that earned Australian soldiers the affection and respect of the people of so many nations. I recognised the men whose virtues the poet celebrated. They were the men I had met in my childhood in Baringhup. The contempt for my mother, which was partly the cause of her failings as much as it was a response to them, was the unattractive side of a conception of value whose other side nourished a distinctively Australian decency. The glories and the miseries of that particular realisation of decency were evident in the men and women of Baringhup and its surroundings.

Around the middle of 1957, my father started writing to a woman in Yugoslavia. Her name was Lydia. She was in her early twenties, tall, slim, dark and very beautiful. He had obtained her address, particulars and photograph from a lonely hearts club especially for Yugoslavs and Romanians.

I do not know why he did this. He was a handsome man and attractive to women, many of whom flirted openly with him, even in my presence. Perhaps it started as a form of amusement but soon it became serious. They wrote at least twice a week and before long there was talk of marriage, and plans for him to bring her, her mother and her brother to Australia. In a culture used to arranged marriages that is not particularly significant. But, as well as intending to marry her, it looked as though he had fallen hopelessly in love with her. The distinction we rightly make between real love and its many false semblances makes me hesitate to say that he actually was in love with her, for, after all, he had never met her. But anyone who saw him, then or later, would have felt an overwhelming inclination to say that he was passionately in love.

I do not remember him more happy. He was young, only thirty-five, strong, respected, joyful in his work, at home with the natural as much as the human world, and he was about to marry a young woman who looked like a film star. His work engrossed him, his business prospered, his friendships flourished. It is small wonder that he was always whistling or singing.

It was a joyful period for me too. It had to do with my father's happiness, but I also had my own reasons. At the beginning of the summer of 1957–58 he allowed me to ride the Bantam, at first only in the paddocks, but later on the roads and eventually to Baringhup. He allowed me because I pestered him daily, but he also had an ulterior motive: he wanted me to collect Lydia's letters from the post office in Baringhup.

Riding the motorbike that summer, through the hot yellow grasslands of central Victoria and around the expansive waters of Cairn Curran, wearing only shorts and sandals, crystallised in me a sense of freedom that I possessed earlier, but never so fully, and which I always associate with that time in the country. I felt I could do anything provided I was respectful of others. The law and other kinds of regulations seemed only rules of thumb, regulative ideals, to be interpreted by individuals according to circumstances and constrained by goodwill and commonsense. From my father and from Hora I had already acquired a sense that only morality was absolute because some of its demands were non-negotiable. But I was too young to be troubled by that. I was eleven years old, riding my father's motorbike to collect the mail and visit friends, yet no one was troubled by this breach of the law. It left me with a sad, haunting image of a freedom, impossible now to realise, and which even then the world could barely afford.

chapter eight

In February of 1958 I went as a boarder to St Patrick's College in Ballarat. It was run by the Christian Brothers, but religion did not figure in my father's reason for sending me there. Dominic Foschia had been there for four years and his parents convinced my father that it was a good school, academically better than anything on offer locally.

I had not seen or heard from my mother since Mitru's funeral. She had placed Susan in a home in

Melbourne where she went to live. Soon after, Barbara was born, in July 1956, four months after her father had killed himself. My mother placed her in a home too. Poor, in money and in health, she lived in various rooming houses and worked mostly as a home helper or kitchen hand. She visited the girls in their different institutions and occasionally had one or both of them to stay with her. She was required to contribute towards their maintenance (in the case of Susan this was £1 10s per week). When she fell behind in her payments she was warned, without compassion or regret, that if she fell four weeks behind, the children would be made wards of the state. This happened towards the end of 1957.

She was very distressed, first at the prospect and then at the fact, that the girls were made wards of the state. But for reasons to do with her nature, and to the extent that it can be separated, with her psychological illness, she was unable to marshal the will to save sufficient money to meet the payments, or even to appear often enough to plead her case. Not that she would have been treated with sympathy if she had. The matron at the Presbyterian Babies Home, where both girls were eventually placed, pending transfer to a Roman Catholic home, declared my mother to be 'a hopeless case' and denied her the right to have her children with her except on weekends, and even that exception was granted grudgingly. Towards the middle of 1958 my mother went again to Ballarat to admit herself as a day-patient at a psychiatric clinic and to work as a polisher in a shoe factory.

One Saturday morning she visited me at school. The headmaster told me only that I had a visitor without telling me who it was, and took me to an empty class-room. I was shocked to see my mother, because I had not seen her for so long and because she looked so unwell, thin and hollow-eyed. She took me into town for lunch. I felt awkward with her and, perhaps to reduce the distance between us, she suggested we play a tune on the jukebox. I chose Buddy Holly singing 'Peggy Sue' and she danced in a cafe half-filled with customers. The pathos of it embarrassed and saddened me.

After we walked back to the school we sat again in the empty classroom where we had met earlier. She told me that she wanted to go back to my father; that she had never loved or respected any man as she had him. Lowering her eyes which had fixed mine with their intensity, she noticed I had a gold chain with a crucifix around my neck. 'Who gave you this?' she demanded, seizing the chain so furiously I thought it would break.

Lydia had, but despite my mother's interrogation I did not admit this.

I did not need to. Her anger told me that she knew it had been given to me by a woman sufficiently intimate to be a threat to my and my father's affection for her. When she resigned herself to the fact that I would not tell her who gave me the chain, she talked again of my father and the past, telling me how deeply she regretted all that had happened. She told me that she was very ill and had been warned by a doctor that she would not live a year unless she was properly cared for.

When my mother left I was deeply disturbed by a sense of her presence and by what she had told me. I also felt resentful that she should have come, just like that, unannounced, after she had neglected even to write to me for almost two and a half years. I asked the headmaster to tell her, if she were to come again, that for the time being I did not want to see her. A week or two later he told me that my mother had come and that he had conveyed my message to her.

When I went home for the holidays in September, I told my father that she had asked to return to him. He told me that it was now impossible, and that, anyhow, it could only end as it had before.

He told her the same when she phoned him. She pleaded with him and he agreed to meet her, but the meeting they arranged never came to pass. She killed herself only days after their conversation.

My father and I were told of her death by the police who came to the Maryborough Show where he was exhibiting his ironwork. I was home, unexpectedly, for a weekend. We packed up and went to Frogmore, neither speaking to the other, each absorbed in his own grief and remorse. That evening I told my father that I wanted my mother to be buried in Maryborough, so the next day we went to Ballarat to arrange the transport of her body and to collect her personal possessions. My father drove the Sunbeam like a man possessed, and when we skidded wildly in some mud he turned to me on the back pillion and said, 'Tomorrow there will be three coffins.' A few kilometres further he took hold of himself and slowed down.

The service was conducted by the local Catholic priest. Remembering Mitru's funeral, my father arranged for the death certificate to state that my mother had died of asphyxiation. This was technically the truth for she had choked on her vomit after taking an overdose of sleeping tablets. As Mitru had done, she lay in an open coffin in Phelan's Funeral Parlour on the morning of the burial. My father asked me if I wanted to see her, this last time.

I said, 'No.' That was all. I could not bear to see her dead and I was too numb to say more.

My father wrote to Maria, my mother's sister, telling her of his grief and guilt and saying, 'In my heart, I still loved her.' Almost thirty years later he told Hora's wife that he never loved a woman as he had my mother.

My father, Hora and, I think, Mitru, did not appreciate the degree to which my mother's life and behaviour were affected by her psychological illness. They seemed to think that she suffered from it only when it was dramatically manifest and necessitated hospitalisation. Yet it must have been present at many stages of her life—certainly when she was unable to get out of bed even to look after her small children.

No doubt we were ignorant of the nature of such illness, as many people still are today. But, looking back, I believe that her behaviour should have seemed stranger than it did to us and to others. No failing of character, no vice, explains or even describes her incapacity properly to care for her children. If one was inclined to say that she was lazy or irresponsible, one would have to qualify it by adding that she was 'pathologically' so. No one is, in any ordinary meaning of these words, lazy or irresponsible to a degree that could adequately capture her incapacity. I suspect something similar was true of her inability to control her spending. Years later, Hora told me that, had he then understood what he now does, he would judge her differently, for he now knows that she could not help herself. I do not know what my father thought, but I know that his demeanour towards her was almost always of someone who saw her more as a helpless cause rather than a free agent of other people's misfortune.

It took many years for my father and me even to begin to resolve our intense and conflicting emotions concerning my mother. For that reason her grave remained without a headstone until 1981 when I came from London and told my father it was time we bought one. It seemed terrible to me that the story of her unhappy and tormented life should include the fact that she lay in an unmarked grave. We were, however, both short of ready cash to pay for a monument, so rather than wait some months my father suggested that we make it ourselves. I happily agreed for I was to return to London within a month and I did not know when we would have another opportunity to remedy what we had so long and shamefully neglected.

In the summer sun we did our remorseful work. We dug the foundations, carried sand from the creek at Carisbrook, mixed the cement and built the monument. My four-year-old daughter, Katie, played among the graves, guaranteeing that we would not yield to morbidity. At one point my father rested on his shovel and cried. 'Memories,' he said.

With shaking hands he rolled a cigarette which he smoked to help control his tears, and he spoke compassionately of my mother's troubled life. Working together, our sorrow lightened by the presence of a young girl representing new life and hope, we came together as son and husband with the woman whose remains lay beneath us.

chapter nine

After my mother died, my father and Hora were especially concerned about the fate of Susan and Barbara. Hora had visited them since they were placed in homes and now did so almost each alternate weekend. He made it clear to the authorities that, although he was not married, he would gladly adopt them, hiring female help to care for them if necessary. Or, if he could not adopt them himself, that he would pay for them to be cared for by another family. He was told that in law he was as nothing to the children.

'But I am their uncle,' he protested.

'I know,' the official replied. He was sympathetic to Hora. 'Biologically you are close to them. Closer than anyone living. And the biological law is deeper than our human law. Still, formalities are formalities. And we go by formalities.' The formalities dragged on for over a year and half.

My father's legal status was more elevated because, although he was not the father of the children and in no other way related to them by blood, he was their mother's husband. Thus, when he let it be known that he wanted to adopt them, he was not rebuffed as quickly as Hora had been. He emphasised that the girls were my sisters and that, although deserted by his wife, he remembered happy times with her and felt obliged to care for her children. His sincerity impressed them and his petition was heard with some interest, particularly as he was able to say that he hoped to marry again within a year or so and that his bride-to-be was willing to care for me and the girls. In addition to the offers of adoption from Hora and my father, approaches came from my mother's German sisters, Maria and Elizabeth.

Despite all this, the authorities preferred to give the girls out for adoption to strangers. Nominally, they kept the door open to my father, asking him to pay a 'regular voluntary contribution for the maintenance of the children' as a sign of good faith and to visit the office again some weeks hence, but it seems that their minds were made up. He did not return as promised and, despite receiving two other letters, did not contact them.

The reason was that he was falling into insanity.

It began in the early autumn of 1960. My father and I went to Melbourne to stay with Hora in Prahran. The year before, my father had bought a white Holden utility from a friend, so we now enjoyed the luxury of travelling without the need of special clothing to protect us from the weather. Hora had only one room, rented to him by Romanian friends of his and my father. Sometimes they were able to offer my father a room, at other times he stayed with other friends nearby, while I stayed with Hora. Sometimes—as on that occasion in 1960— the three of us slept in one bed.

My father had heard that a woman had arrived in Melbourne who had known Lydia and, of course, he wanted to meet her. With Hora he went to the western outskirts of Melbourne where she lived. He told her of his hopes and plans: the immigration formalities had at last been completed. Lydia, her mother and brother were now free to come to Australia and he had bought land in Maryborough and commissioned an architect to build a fine new brick house.

She listened appalled, with evident pity for him. She

told him to lay aside his plans. Lydia was not the woman he imagined her to be. On no account should he trust her. He must write to her and demand she tell him the truth.

I was not with my father and Hora when they visited the woman whose news would change the course of my father's life. When I returned to Prahran after swimming at the city baths, my father was lying on Hora's bed, moaning in heart-rending distress. Hora told me he had severe stomach trouble. This was half true. On the return journey with Hora he felt nauseated and weak from shock and his stomach began to cramp. But I knew that could only be some of the truth, for my father's face was tortured in ways that I knew instinctively no mere physical ailment could explain. When we drove home to Frogmore that night my father told me nothing of the cause of his anguish. We arrived well after midnight. I went to bed. He wrote to Lydia.

For the next few days, until I went back to boarding school, my father did not go to work. He slept until late in the morning and in the afternoon would search through documents and read Lydia's old letters. After I had dinner—he ate none himself—he began to write to Lydia and continued until the early hours of the morning. From the bedroom, I saw his hunched shadow cast large against the kitchen wall by the light of the kerosene lamp. Again and again, I heard him tear the paper from the writing pad, begin to write, crush it and throw it on the floor. Each time he sighed more deeply than I had ever heard anyone sigh, and I heard in those sighs the terrible depths of his suffering. They have become for me the haunting emblem of his affliction.

My father's vulnerability changed my attitude to Frogmore. In his sighs I heard our isolation and for the first time I felt estranged from the area. I was also in a state of confusion caused by two irreconcilable emotions. The joys of my freedom over the last year and a half whenever I was at Frogmore were still intense to me, and made more poignant by my premonition that I would never experience them again. But my father's talk of marriage and building a new house in Maryborough had awakened in me a desire to live what I began to think of as a normal life, desirable just because it was the kind of life lived or sought by almost everyone I knew.

Lydia and my father had now been writing to each other for over two years. Every so often she included an affectionate note to me to which I responded. I had become guiltily fond of her and uneasy with my desire that she be my father's wife. My growing desire to lead a 'normal' life was strengthened by the conformist aspirations of teenage culture, which tempted me to betray the gift of my freedom for the suburban life of

Maryborough; to exchange Cairn Curran for the Maryborough swimming pool where, as I once told Hora, I thought 'atmosphere' was to be found. Derision was his apt response, but the worm was already in the apple.

It took days for my father to finish and post his letter to Lydia. After he had done so he wrote at least one letter a day for the next fortnight. Sometimes he demanded the truth from her. At other times he pleaded for it. When Lydia finally replied, nothing could have prepared him for what she told him. She had a husband whom she had married only weeks earlier, after a long engagement.

My father was thrown into confusion. He could not deny the facts and showed no inclination to do so. The character of his bewilderment came not from the question, did she really do it?, nor from the question, why did she do it? It came from the question, how could she have done it?, which of its nature ruled out any answer, persisting independently of any facts he might accept concerning her motives and circumstances.

His bewilderment—posed as a question, but accepting no answers—was of a kind common to betrayed and grieving lovers. It is also a common response to certain kinds of wrongdoing and to the death of those dear to us, when no facts of a natural or supernatural kind will diminish our pained bewilderment at the disappearance of a human personality.

Yet there was another dimension to my father's confusion, and it proved the most damaging. Morality was for him as substantially a part of reality as the natural facts of human action and motivation, but when Lydia's letter arrived his moral world collapsed. Despite what he had seen and had personally suffered, his moral world was coloured by an innocence which had not been threatened by the wrongs done to him by my mother and Mitru, because he knew them to be as much victims as agents in a drama that was to consume them.

His compassionate fatalism could not, however, accommodate Lydia's mendacity. It could accept many forms of folly, weakness and vice, but not a malevolent human will. Of course he had the concept of such a will, but it was weak in him, an abstraction, never a living reality. Believing himself to be directly confronted with it in the person of a woman he loved and had trusted without reservation, his personal disintegration followed not far behind the disintegration of his moral world.

His sense of life, before Lydia's betrayal, is beautifully expressed in the 'Prayer for the Dead' in *The Book of Common Prayer*. 'Man that is born of woman hath but a short time to live and is full of misery. He cometh up and is cut down like a flower. He fleeth as it were a shadow and never continueth in one stay.' Those accents of sorrow and pity determined his sense of all other human beings as his fellow mortals, victims of fate and destined for suffering. They determined the quality of his deeply felt compassion in which all his moral judgments were embedded. But, after Lydia's betrayal, his intense sense of a malevolent will could never become for him just another appalling fact to be added to his knowledge of human nature. It always bewildered him that such a thing could exist, and he responded to it in different ways, sometimes angrily, sometimes bitterly, sometimes sorrowfully, but never with resignation.

Only someone with an extraordinary sense of the reality of the ethical could be so shaken by a sense of evil, and my father was such a person. I believe it is why he seldom sang or whistled again and that, when he did, it was never with the same innocent pleasure as before.

In September 1960, he admitted himself as a voluntary patient to the Ballarat psychiatric hospital. I first knew of it when I came to Melbourne to stay with Hora in my holidays from Puckapunyal, an army camp in central Victoria where I had been on cadet camp. Camp had been enjoyable and I looked forward to a week in Melbourne before going on to Frogmore. Concerned at how I would respond, Hora broke the news gently and with a tenderness that assured me of comfort if I were to fall to pieces.

Though it came as no surprise, because I knew my father was threatened by insanity, the news was a shock, one that deepened when Hora and I visited my father in hospital.

The hospital represented a foreign world to me, one whose beliefs were shaped by ideas I instinctively felt to be in conflict with those that had enabled me to understand the events of my childhood. I could no longer see my father's illness just from the perspective of our life at Frogmore. Strange though it may sound, my sense of that life, of the ideas that informed it, was given intensity and colour by the light and land-scape of the area. The hills looked as old as the earth, because they were rounded by millennia and also because the grey and equally rounded granite boulders that stood among the long yellow grasses, sharply delineated at all times of day by the summer sun, made them look prehistoric. More than anything, however, the glorious, tall, burnt-yellow grasses (as a boy they came to my chest and sometimes over my head) moving irregularly against a deep blue sky, dominated the images of my childhood and gave colour to my freedom and also to my understanding of suffering. In the morning they inspired cheerful energy of the kind that made you whistle; at midday, in partnership with an unforgiving sun and alive with insects and other creatures, they intimidated; but in

the late afternoon, towards dusk, everything was soft-
ened by a light that graced the area in a melancholy
beauty that could pierce one's soul, as it did mine on
the day I went in search of rabbits, and many times
thereafter.

Religion, metaphysics or the notions of fate and
character as they inform tragedy are suited to that
light and landscape. The assumptions of psychiatric
medicine, affected as they are by psychiatry's debunk-
ing of metaphysics in its long struggle to become
accepted as a science, were not. Life at Frogmore, in
that landscape and under that light, nourished the
sense given to me by my father and Hora, of the
contrast between the malleable laws and conventions
made by human beings to reconcile and suit their
many interests, and the uncompromising authority of
morality, always the judge, never merely the servant
of our interests.

For that reason tragedy, with its calm pity for the
affliction it depicts, was the genre that first attracted
my passionate allegiance: I recognised in it the concepts that had illuminated the events of my childhood.
They enabled me to see Mitru, my mother, my father
and Vacek, living among his boulders, as the victims
of misfortune, in their different ways broken by it,
but never thereby diminished.

That is why my heart broke when I saw my father

in the ward before he saw us, in a room full of visibly disturbed people, some obviously insane, and he shrunken and bewildered. He had been given shock treatment and was one of those who felt it as a humiliating assault. Not everyone feels that way, but many do even when they concede that it is necessary. His pitiable state was increased by the effects of large doses of Largactil.

He had not been expecting us and greeted us with surprised hesitation, ambivalent about my presence, pleased but mortified and, I think, humiliated. He protested that he was fine, that he was not really ill because he could 'speak normally' whenever he made the effort. I suspect he was quite oblivious to the pathos in that claim, because he repeated it many times to protest that he was not as ill as he might appear to be.

I left the hospital changed. I had absorbed past sorrows against the sure confidence of my father's strength. I knew that, whatever was to come, I could never do so again.

I stayed a fortnight or so with Hora, but my father's insanity cast its shadow over everything I did or thought. I did not see him again until I came home to Frogmore for the summer holidays. He had released himself from hospital almost two months before, and his paranoia was feverish. To protect me he tried to hide the signs of insanity as much as he could but it was impossible, for they were always visible and sometimes spectacular.

Once, on the verandah, I saw his eyes wide with terror, his body trembling because he believed he could see a sheet of flame rise from the concrete and threaten to engulf both of us. He made wooden and iron crosses to ward off evil spirits and, when he cut the bread, he first crossed it with the knife. He questioned me without respite about the meaning of almost everything I did—why had I put the fork, the matches, my shoes just there, why did I stand or sit here rather than there, why did I write, say or wear this rather than that, and so on, relentlessly.

There seemed to be no reason why he would single out some kinds of things rather than others. Anything slightly out of the ordinary was potentially a sign. They were of different kinds. Some were superstitions he learned in Yugoslavia. If an owl hooted it meant someone would die. He swore an owl hooted three times when my mother died. If his left eye beat it meant bad luck for someone. Always he feared for someone else, most often for me, but never for himself.

He also invented elaborate and convoluted signs. Sometimes he would see five of something and connect it, via some intermediary occurrence, with the fact that 'Gaita' has five letters. Sometimes an English sound would be similar to the sound of a word in Romanian or German, and it would trigger a thought connected with the meaning of the word in those languages. Or he would focus on the number of letters in the word rather than its sound. The ingenuities of his associations left one with few means of escape from his anxious and sometimes aggressive attentions.

Over time, by carefully doing nothing in ways that were even slightly out of the ordinary, I learned to minimise the extent to which I would provoke his anxiety, but such strategies were only partially successful against the resourceful manoeuvres of his paranoia. This was hard for me to bear, as it was for anyone in frequent contact with him. For him it was terrifying, not because he feared what would happen to him, but because he feared that he would drive away evil forces only for them to turn their fury on those he loved and who were less able to withstand their assault. To prevent this he had some months earlier tried to kill himself with an overdose of Largactil. By chance Tom Lillie came to the house at just that time to ask him to weld a broken gate, found him unconscious and took him to hospital.

He was a passionate man and his madness was passionate. Its intensity became unbearable for me, and so for my own sake as well as his I urged him to go to hospital. He would not go. He said that he could not because the Christmas deliveries of his work were due, that they were the culmination of his year's work and that a failure to deliver would cost him money and also, more seriously, his reputation. All this was true, but it did not really explain the quality of his refusal which was as ferocious as other aspects of his illness.

We were arguing in the living room, next to Vacek's room. Vacek had returned to help my father in his work. Far from sane himself, he joined me in urging my father to go, at first hesitantly but soon energetically, partly because the extent of my father's illness was evident even to him, and partly because he saw it as an opportunity to free himself from my father's relentless demands. My father was becoming desperate. He moved backwards away from us. We followed him and this must have appeared threatening to him because he picked up an axe and swore that he would cut our heads off if we came closer.

Perhaps nothing indicates so clearly my sense of the seriousness of his illness than the fact that I was neither surprised nor dismayed. Not so my father. Within a few seconds, badly shaken by the realisation of what he was doing, he put down the axe, agreeing to go to hospital, on condition that he drive himself.

Exacting this condition was important to his self-respect because it enabled him to believe that he still had some control over events, and for the same reason it was important to him that he admit himself as a voluntary patient rather than being taken forcibly and certified. He telephoned Jack Matthey, the policeman in Maldon, who came and accompanied him while my father drove to Ballarat. Matthey brought the car home and told me to put the keys away.

I had promised my father that one way or another I would deliver his ironwork before Christmas. This was important, for financial reasons—we needed the money—for his reputation and also for his sense that things were not entirely out of control. His feeling, that he had delegated a task justifiably confident that it could be carried out, would be undermined if he had serious reason to think that I could not succeed in it. He therefore needed to be convinced that the physical means to do it were at my disposal, and also, even more importantly, that I could survive psychologically, a fourteen-year-old boy who had suffered considerable trauma, alone with only Vacek for a companion.

To convince him I telephoned a school friend in Warrnambool asking him if he would come to Baringhup to help me. Amazingly he said that he would. Unsatisfactory as it would have been in other circumstances, this had to satisfy my father. It was a compromise between his need seriously to be convinced that I could deliver and his reluctant acknowledgment that he had to go to hospital.

My school friend's name was John Dunstan. His generosity deserves more than its mere recording, so I will say something of his short, sad life. An orphan, his uncle paid for him to live with family friends who cared for him with kindness and treated him as one of the family. His mother had committed suicide when he was a baby. He had two uncles, one poor, but kind and ineffectual, who spent his time fishing supported by the second uncle who was wealthy and brutish, but who, when all was said and done, fulfilled his responsibilities to John and was more than generous to his brother who appeared never to have seriously felt an obligation to work.

John was wild and melancholic in turns, and at school was a loner, which was part of what attracted me to him. Neither academically gifted nor inclined, he left school after fifth form to work in a bank in Warrnambool. When I first went to university, I foolishly persuaded him to leave his job and to complete his secondary education in Melbourne so that he could go to university. He came to Melbourne, failed his matriculation, became lost and unstable and, four years later, jumped to his death from the housing commission flats in Carlton.

But these terrible events were in the future. A week

before Christmas, I met John at Maryborough station in my father's utility which I had learnt to drive six months or so before, sometimes with my father and sometimes by myself. He would leave the car parked outside the house and walk through the paddock to work at Lillie's. The keys were always in the ignition, so I would start it and drive it for short distances along the track. This way I learnt the gears and clutch control and, by the time my father decided to teach me, to his astonishment I needed only to practise steering on the roads. When John and I arrived at Frogmore, I took some pleasure in his amazement when he saw the outside of the house, and his even greater amazement when he saw inside.

We left his suitcase at Frogmore and drove to Lillie's to assess our task—the delivery within ten days or so of a couple of hundred garden settings and other items such as tables and magazine racks. My father had made high steel sidings to be attached to the tray of the utility, so that goods could be stacked to one and a half times its height, but, even so, we would need to do many trips. We sized up our task, lifting tables and chairs in order to assess how heavy they were, but also as a ritual to reassure ourselves and to placate the gods in case they suspected us of hubris. We agreed that we could do it and, for the first time since I had promised my father, I actually felt confident that we could.

Dark had fallen by the time we came back to Frogmore. I lit the lamp and heated soup on the primus. Within moments of sitting down to talk we heard noises from the next room. Vacek had woken. He was asleep when we first arrived so John had not seen him, and I had forgotten both to tell John about him and that I hadn't told him. I saw that John was a little anxious, but I assumed that was because he was alone with me in semi-darkness, in the primitive surroundings of Frogmore, kilometres from anywhere.

Then we heard footsteps coming towards the kitchen and, before I realised the cause and extent of John's fright, Vacek appeared at the kitchen door. Under his chin he held a kerosene lamp which partially illuminated his fully bearded face making it appear to float free of his body which was in darkness. His fearsome appearance was aggravated by his expression of confused irritation and by the fact that sleep had made his hair wild. John jumped under the table.

Sensing himself to be the cause of this extraordinary event, but confused, because he didn't know who John was, because he could not understand why he should cause such a reaction in anyone, and because he was anyhow a little mad, Vacek put the lamp on the table and peered under it, muttering apologies and explanations, none of which made much sense. Nor, I suspect, did John hear any of it because, at the sight of Vacek's head under the table, he ran out of the house into the darkness of the paddock. It took hours for him to settle.

After we made the first delivery without him, Vacek realised that we had no real need of him and went, I do not know where. I was sad to see him go; I felt for him as though he were part of my family, but I also knew that such coming and going was part of his nature. And it was true that he was not needed. He could have helped load and unload the utility, but it would have saved us only an hour or two each time. John and I managed by ourselves and completed all our deliveries to Myer stores in Ballarat, Bendigo and Geelong within a day or two of the dates my father had promised.

Our duty done, John and I were restless. We were teenagers with no desire to spend our time at Frogmore, swimming or reading, although in the event we did quite a lot of that. We drove around aimlessly, to Maryborough and other towns, sometimes racing local lads in the utility at speeds that should have killed us all. One night we drove to Castlemaine where we took a room at a hotel, hoping to bring girls there. Although we had in the car and the hotel room trappings of sophistication well beyond our age, we had little more and we had no idea how actually to go about getting the girls we lusted after. We spent a forlorn Christmas day, searching without luck for anything that looked like a public celebration we could join.

When Jack Matthey's blue Holden arrived at Frogmore our travelling came to an end. On the previous day workmen had been tarring the road to Baringhup, both sides at once. Before I quite realised what I was doing, I drove through their work at speed, spraying them with tar. In the rear-vision mirror I saw them shaking their fists. John and I raised our thumbs in return. That evening they filed a report at the Maldon police station.

When he came it was clear that Matthey had known for some time that I had been driving. He had decided to turn a blind eye because he knew that my father was in hospital and that, in the beginning at least, I was driving in order to complete his deliveries. Now I had forced his hand; he had no alternative. He told me that I had been an idiot, took the car keys and left it at that. I was astonished that he had not arrested me, for he had a fearsome reputation for seeking out law-breakers and for mercilessly enforcing the letter of the law against them.

A few months later he caught me driving again. Furious that I had not been deterred by his warning, and perhaps because I had abused his generosity, he threatened to see me and my father in jail. When the case came before the children's court in Maldon,

Matthey pleaded on our behalf, saying that this was a case of 'good people doing the wrong thing', that I was a poor boy who had to ride a bicycle four miles to get an ice-cream, that my father was a good hardworking man and so on. I was fined one pound for driving, my father two pounds for letting me and the magistrate said no conviction would be recorded. I am sure that we owed this generosity to Matthey's plea on our behalf. His normally fearsome reputation served us well.

When my father came home from hospital in midJanuary, John returned to Warrnambool. Vacek also came home—for by then that is what Frogmore was to him—and he and my father began working again. The stores had sold out of garden settings and had placed urgent orders for more. He was far from cured of his illness: his paranoia, his disposition to see omens everywhere, even his hallucinations persisted, but nothing seemed so fierce as before, about to consume him and everyone around him. Relief lasted only a few weeks, however, and I thought it an ominous sign when he asked me to cut his hair completely off.

A few weeks later he visited me at school in Ballarat with Vacek. As soon as I saw him I knew that his illness had again overtaken him. He came dressed in a dishevelled navy pin-striped suit, with a dirty white shirt open at the neck, the collar partly covered by the collar of his jacket. He seemed shrunken, stooped, not with age (he was only thirty-nine), but with the burden of his affliction. Most startling was his face: thin, unshaven, his eyes, not dead as is often the case with depression, but burning with the terror of his visions, all made worse by the fact that his almost shaven head made him look as though he had come from a concentration camp.

Vacek walked beside him in an equally shabby beige suit and an open dirty shirt, wearing, as ever, his beanie. He no longer had a beard, and his open, amiable face was covered in stubble. His eyes focused on no one, his lips were hardly ever still, moving in sometimes silent, sometimes audible conversation with himself or imaginary partners. Afterwards a teacher asked me if one of the men had been my father. 'No,' I replied. I was later tormented with guilt and shame for having denied my father, but I knew not quite for what I was ashamed because I also knew that, terrible though it was, my denial was not prompted by cowardice.

I do not know what set my father on the very long road to recovery. He singles out an event that occurred while I was with him during the May holidays of 1961.

'Come Raimond,' he said to me late one afternoon. 'We're going to Sydney.'

'Why?' I asked, surprised at the suddenness of this announcement.

He hesitated for a moment and then said, 'I'm going to shoot him.'

I knew he meant Lydia's husband. He and Lydia had come to Sydney only months before. My father's mind was made up and I knew that nothing I could do or say would change it. Lamely, I asked whether he thought it a good idea. He dismissed my question with a contemptuous grunt and gesture of his hand.

I was not morally appalled by what my father was setting out to do. Mitru's suicide and my father's madness had convinced me that sexual love was a passion whose force and nature was mysterious, and that anyone who came under its sway should be prepared to be destroyed by it. Its capacity to wreck lives, to humiliate otherwise strong and proud people and to drive them to suicide was already familiar to me. That it should also drive them to murder was part of the same story.

I had long felt that a person passionately in love was in the grip of something whose imperatives required one to accept, without complaint, that one might be murdered by a grief-stricken or jealous lover. The requirement to consent to such possibilities seemed to me to be intrinsic to love's nature and, therefore, inseparable from its joys. To my mind that requirement constituted the very essence of this awesome passion. I believed, moreover, that Lydia's cold-blooded mendacity was contemptible in a way that my father's intention to kill her husband, and perhaps her, was not. Not that I believed that this would justify my father if he killed them. I did not believe they deserved to die—certainly not at anyone else's hand, and not even at my father's. For me it was never a question of justification. I simply refused to condemn my father for intending to shoot Lydia's husband.

That refusal was not conditional on him being my father. I would have refused to condemn anyone in a similar position to his, and I would have thought any victim of such a killing to be unworthy of their passion if they complained. The fact that he was my father was the reason I felt obliged to accompany him. It never occurred to me to say I would not go. But I also accepted that he might quite rightly pay the legal penalty, go to jail and perhaps even be hanged for murder.

We shared the driving and arrived at Lydia's house early in the morning, around seven o'clock. My father said that we should wait until a more suitable time before knocking at their door. This courtesy struck me as incongruous with our purpose, and I did not know whether to take it as a sign that my father had abandoned his plan, or that his natural courtesy showed through even when he was intent on murder.

We waited almost two hours before we knocked on the door. Lydia opened it. She was even more beautiful than her photographs, gentle in every movement and in her speech, as delicate in manner as in her tall, slim, graceful figure. It was impossible to see the wickedness in her. Her husband was also gentle and courteous. His courtesy must have disarmed my father, but it was her beauty that saved him from death and my father from becoming a murderer. There were no shots, not even very angry words. I do not know what they talked about for they spoke in Yugoslav, which I did not understand. After some hours of talk my father and I set off for home.

I was profoundly relieved when we went because I had fully expected to spend that evening in a children's home while my father was sent to prison. But as deep as my relief was, so was my pity for my father because of his suffering and humiliated love for this beautiful woman.

On the road home we passed some cliffs on a hillside a kilometre or so from the road. They caught my interest and I looked at them for some time. Years later my father told me he thought I intended to indicate to him that he would do me and others a service if he went to those cliffs and jumped off. He said that, because I could not be blamed for wishing it, he found in his shame the strength to begin the long haul to recovery.

I have seldom seen such affliction as I saw my father suffer in those last years in Frogmore, and I only saw it again when I worked as a student in psychiatric hospitals. He understood it before he became its victim. Some years before, while we were travelling on the motorbike, he talked about Vacek and said, 'There is no sickness worse than mental sickness.'

I remember his words clearly. I remember the exact point where we were on the road. Most of all, I remember his strong, bare, sun-darkened arms on either side of me as I sat on the petrol tank. For me to remember his words and our surroundings so vividly, the authority with which he spoke them must have impressed me deeply. The sight of his muscular arms protected me against their terrible meaning.

chapter ten

During the severe period of his illness my father quarrelled with many of his friends and also with those he employed to work for him.

After electric welding, a thin metal crust forms over the weld which needs to be removed before painting. This is done first by grinding and then by cleaning off the residue with a steel brush. Stan Smolak came from Maldon to grind the welding residue from the garden settings and to help my father when he was painting.

My father would question him as to why he had done something this way rather than that, and often whatever Smolak said in reply provoked my father to anxious and paranoid outbursts.

He sometimes refused to work because he believed that omens told him not to. On one occasion Smolak arrived at the workshop, but not finding my father there he went to Frogmore in search of him. There he found him in bed. My father told Smolak that Jack had scratched a certain pattern in the dirt which meant that he had scratched away that day's work. 'No work today,' my father said. He paid Smolak his petrol money and went back to bed.

Eventually even the equitable Vacek had had enough, and one day when my father, quite reasonably on this occasion, asked him to grind the welding res-idues in a particular way, Vacek threw down the grinder and declared he was leaving. Despite my father's plea that he wait at least until the end of the week, Vacek refused to stay another hour. He went home to Frog-more, packed his entire belongings in a small bag and set off on his motorbike, this time never to return.

He wandered from town to town, and for a while returned to his boulders outside Maldon. But times had become less tolerant since he had first lived there seven years earlier, and the police took him to the Ballarat psychiatric hospital, where he became a certified patient for no better reason than that he lived between boulders, talked to himself and sometimes cooked food in his urine. Over time he became dependent on institutional living so that, even when he was free to leave, he preferred to stay, and remained there and in reception homes in the community for the rest of his life.

Hora also quarrelled with my father. After Mitru died he went to Sydney in the hope that physical distance from the tragedy would enable him to find the emotional distance he needed to come to terms with it. It was not to be. In Sydney he met and fell deeply but unhappily in love with a young woman whom he hoped to marry. She refused him because she had had one lung removed, diseased with tuberculosis. She feared the recurrence of her illness, that she would be unable to have children and that she would therefore bring only sorrow to the man she married. Hora protested without success. He had no choice but to accept her resolve not to burden him with marriage to an invalid.

My father told me that the pain of this loss affected Hora for years. He always spoke of it in a tone which expressed sorrow for Hora and his awe at our vulnerability to affliction.

Absorbed in his sorrows, Hora had his patience severely tried by my father who sometimes regarded him as a kind of chief wizard in a complicated play of supernatural forces. Although this was a backhanded expression of my father's admiration for him, Hora was understandably hurt to be cast in this role. Realising how much his presence disturbed my father, Hora suggested that they see less of each other and they were estranged for almost two years. They also quarrelled over something more serious.

Soon after my father had been released from his first stay at the Ballarat psychiatric hospital, he received a letter calling him to Melbourne to discuss urgently the fate of Susan and Barbara. He was in fact called to consent to their adoption. Realising there was now no hope that he, Hora or any other members of the family could adopt the girls, he signed a letter of consent, pleading that Hora and I have access to them. Because he had no legal standing, Hora was not present and his consent was not sought.

Despite my father's claim that he could 'speak normally' whenever he set his mind to it, it must have been evident to the authorities at the children's home that they were asking for the signature of a highly disturbed man whom they knew had been released from a psychiatric hospital only a couple of months before. Yet it is clear from the official papers that they were determined to obtain his signature if at all possible. The fact that this signature, extracted from a person who was mentally ill, was of doubtful legal standing was, I suppose, a risk they thought worth taking, predicting that my father would not cause trouble over it later.

After he signed the papers, my father went to visit Hora in Prahran. Hora was bitterly unhappy about the adoption. Partly because of previous tensions, and partly because of the drink with which he tried to ease his sorrows, he quarrelled angrily with my father because my father had given his consent without any assurance that those who intended to adopt the girls would agree to allow them to see him, Hora or me.

Hora knew that access was at the discretion of the adopting couple. Previously, when a couple had sought to adopt the girls, they allowed him to visit them on weekends when they had them for trial periods. The couple assured Hora that if they were permitted to adopt the girls they would welcome his visits and mine. But the girls were transferred to a Roman Catholic home and, because both the husband and wife were Anglicans, they were refused permission to adopt them.

Hora was very fond of the girls. He visited them regularly and was deeply distressed by their plight, Susan's in particular because she repeatedly banged her head against the wall or against the bedstead at night. On the day they were adopted, he went to see them for the last time. He stood with them waiting for the car to take them away. When it arrived, the girls were rushed inside, and the people who adopted them neither greeted Hora nor said farewell to him. They offered not a word of reassurance or sympathy, though they knew who he was and how often he had visited them.

He was left standing at the kerb as they sped off and did not see the girls again until over thirty years later when I tracked them down.

Despite their quarrels, Hora and my father remained friends, but friends apart. This was because of the strength of old bonds, because Hora knew that it was my father's illness that caused him to act as he did, but mostly because Hora knew that, despite his illness, there was still no one who remained as steadfast as my father in his disdain of superficialities, in his honesty and in his concern for others. Though he was often impossible to be with, and provoked quarrels with almost anyone who was not a saint, his essential character remained untouched by his illness. Later, when his illness relaxed its grip and he was in control of the imaginings which still afflicted him, but which he did not voice so aggressively or with such anguish, their friendship revived.

My father seldom properly understood his part in their quarrels, which was not surprising given the seriousness of his illness. But his lack of self-knowledge about this was complicated by something that became evident to me only later, because it needed to be isolated from his illness in order to be fully visible. He often defended himself against someone's anger by saying that all he did or said was such and such, whereupon there followed an account of what he had said or done which was both inaccurate and in his favour. He was not lying. I never knew my father to lie. He was deceiving himself and, although the phenomenon is commonplace, in him it was puzzling because he appeared to lack the concept of self-deception entirely.

At first his illness disguised this from me. But even after I knew that his illness could not explain this curious untruthfulness of a scrupulously honest man, it took some years for me to understand this aspect of my father. Despite the paradoxical nature of the fact that the same person can simultaneously be deceiver and deceived, the concept of self-deception goes so deep in our culture that it never occurred to me that anyone might simply not possess it. When I realised that my father did not, it added pathos to his self-deception, but also made it more frustrating because I knew that I was powerless in the face of it. When once I told him that there were other ways of being untruthful than by lying, that one might be untruthful to oneself, he clearly had no idea what I was talking about and could find no familiar conceptual path to doing so.

In a man for whom truthfulness mattered so much, this was a pathetic state of affairs. I have already remarked how both my father and Hora looked upon prudential justifications of truthfulness and other virtues as demeaning of our humanity. They did not value truthfulness for its usefulness. They valued it because, to adapt the words of a fine English philosopher, they were men for whom *not to falsify* had become a spiritual demeanour.

By the middle of 1962 I convinced my father to accept an offer to buy a modest weatherboard house from a friend in Maryborough. I suspect that I succeeded in convincing him because he knew in his heart that he would never build the house he had intended for Lydia, although the plans were drawn up, the bricks were all on site and the foundations dug. Nothing now prevented him from engaging the bricklayers, whom he knew and who had agreed to do it. Sensing that he had a psychological block against it, I pestered him to buy a house until eventually he did.

Perhaps he shouldn't have because, although he lived in it until he died, he never cared for it, feeling always that he would have preferred to live in a house he built himself, while never according that preference sufficient weight to act on it. I think that long before he articulated it to himself and others, he felt that it was an indulgence to build a better house when he lived in one that was adequate. That feeling expressed an austerity which became deeper and more pervasive over time.

As he grew older it became clear that the house he had bought was not only adequate, it suited his spartan disposition much better than a new house in which he would have seemed incongruous. It was small, with two bedrooms and a sleep-out on the verandah, but it had a very deep backyard looking out onto forest. He kept animals in the backyard and grew all manner of vegetables. Although the house was on the outskirts of Maryborough and surrounded by other houses, when one looked through the kitchen window one could easily imagine oneself to be in the bush.

Something besides my pestering was at work in prompting my father to buy a house in Maryborough, and at the same time to make him disinclined to build the one he had intended for Lydia. Her mother and brother were soon to arrive in Australia. Their fares were paid not by Lydia and her husband, but by my father. He had promised to do it years before, and it was inconceivable that he would go back on his word, whatever Lydia had done to him and irrespective of whether her mother and her brother had been accomplices in her deception. Even if he had discovered that Lydia's mother had urged her to lie to him, that they had concocted the whole scheme, he would not have gone back on his word. He had promised and that was binding on him. If they wanted to come he would bring them.

Of course they did want to come.

They arrived in Maryborough just before the end of 1962. She was an attractive, dark, middle-aged woman, who spoke almost no English. He was tall and good-looking like Lydia, educated, eighteeen or nineteen, and spoke a reasonable English that rapidly improved during his time in Maryborough. I am afraid that their names have completely escaped my memory. She stayed at home in the house while he quickly found a job as a typesetter at a local printing house. I felt no resentment towards either of them. Because I had already seen a fair number of unusual things, a slightly bizarre twist to the tale of my father's life came as no surprise to me. Also, my childhood had prepared me to accept what came, as much for reasons of prudence as of virtue.

In fact, I had little to do with Lydia's mother and whatever reservations I had were overcome by my pleasure at a feminine presence in the house. They were both kind to me, and the brother especially took pains to spend time with me. He spoke to me for hours about the evils of communism, of the heroes of the Yugoslav and Hungarian resistance, and indicated that he would try to join Australian movements dedicated to over-throwing the communist government of Yugoslavia.

From the outset it was clear that Lydia's mother

hoped that my father would marry *her* and, indeed, that she was confident he would. She did not believe that he would have brought her and her son to Australia merely to keep his word, and so it must have seemed to her highly probable that, because he was lonely and seeking a wife, he would settle for the mother instead of her daughter. She was, after all, only a few years older than my father who had just turned forty. According to the criteria that determine prospects in arranged marriages, she would have been a good catch. Still attractive in middle age, with considerable charm, she worked hard in the house and cooked and cleaned. My father said on more than one occasion that she was a good woman who would make a good wife—only not for him.

She had no sense of his desperate passion for Lydia. Perhaps she believed him to be as insincere as her daughter and that he persisted in the strange romance with Lydia for reasons other than those he declared. My father unintentionally but naively encouraged her belief in her prospects when he allowed her to choose furniture suites for the bedrooms and living room, which stayed in the house until he died. I doubt that my father felt ambivalent, but his behaviour gave her cause to hope even though he told her many times that she had no grounds for it and should nurse no ambitions of marriage.

And so it remained, more or less, for a few months. Though by no means completely well, my father had improved considerably. He worked hard, still at Lillie's, for he had not built or bought a new workshop in Maryborough. He continued to see signs in many things, and sometimes interrogated people about what they had said or done. Occasionally he erupted in irrational behaviour, but on the whole he kept his imaginings sufficiently clear of his behaviour to lead something resembling a normal life.

On the eve of the new year 1963, an old friend of my father's came to Maryborough. To protect his identity, I shall call him 'M'. My father was glad to see him because he had offended M during his illness and they had seen little of each other since. M arrived while I was out and had been celebrating with my father for a few hours by the time I returned. Hearing the conversation before I entered the room, I felt that everything was just as it had been years before. They were in fine spirits, talking as they had in the past, with animated intensity, with pleasure and laughter. Lydia's mother joined in. Homemade *slivovitz*, up to 90 per cent proof, flowed freely.

M slept with me in a small room on the verandah. Around three in the morning I heard him get up to go to the lavatory and noticed that he was gone a long time. I thought he might be sick after so much to drink, but because I was only partly awake I fell asleep before he returned. The next morning I woke before him and went into the house to hear my father speaking on the telephone in an agitated voice. When I asked him what was the matter, he told me that he had phoned the hospital to see if a psychiatrist could come to the house; Lydia's mother had gone mad. She was saying that M had come to her bed that night. She refused to get up until he left the house.

Remembering the events of the previous night, I suspected she was not at all mad. When M came into the kitchen minutes after me, he told my incredulous father that Lydia's mother's story was essentially true. After he went to the lavatory he went to her room. It was pitch-black, with no streetlights, no moon and no other light to relieve the darkness. When he came into her bed she received him with evident pleasure.

Only afterwards, when he spoke, did she realise who he was. In the darkness she had thought he was my father, and that her hopes had finally materialised. When she discovered that it was M who had made love to her, she threw him out of bed quietly, so as not to wake my father, reserving her hysteria for the morning.

My father listened to M with mixed emotions that were written clearly across his face. He was amused, it was so evidently a terrific story. But, though he was amused by the plot, he wished the story had a different setting. He showed no anger towards M for he knew that M would not have dreamed of going to the disconsolate woman's bed if my father had not persistently said that he had no interest whatsoever in her, or if he knew how firmly she would have been opposed to his advances. M believed she had given him some encouragement during the evening of drinking and conversation in the kitchen, and took her willingness as a further expression of it. After all, the truth —that she had mistaken him for my father—was so improbable that it would not have occurred to him to be the reason why she consented to his lovemaking.

Lydia's mother accused my father of putting M up to it and said that she would not rise from her bed until M left the house. The requirements of hospitality were profoundly important to my father and he was fully aware of what it meant for him to ask a friend to leave his house, even in these circumstances. On the other hand, he knew Lydia's mother had a case and was, anyway, troubled by what to do if she made good her threat not to get out of bed. In the event M spared him the decision and went without being asked.

She left too a month or so later to join her son who had gone to Sydney in pursuit of work more suited to his intellectual gifts. She parted on speaking terms with my father and indeed, later that year, I stayed with her for a few days when I went to Sydney, to get a driver's licence a year earlier than the law in Victoria allowed. But that was the last we heard of her or her daughter.

By this time—I was almost sixteen—my relationship with my father had changed because I had asserted my independence. It occasioned a fierce but short-lived quarrel between us. He believed strongly that if you started something then you should finish it. He took this attitude when I told him that I intended to leave boarding school in Ballarat. It was early in the school year and I had been threatened with expulsion. Hora had often mentioned Bertrand Russell to me with admiration, so when in my second last year of secondary schooling I decided I would be a schoolteacher, I read Russell's book on education. I was much impressed with his views, including his views on sex education, and expressed my enthusiasm for them to my classmates. The headmaster got to hear of this and threatened me with expulsion on the grounds that I was corrupting them.

A week or so later the headmaster noticed that I was wearing fashionably pointed-toed shoes. They were banned in the school, but my only other pair was being mended. He told me to take them off immediately. We were in the dining room at lunchtime, so I assumed he meant that I could put them on again when I had finished eating. It was raining and cold outside. As I was running to class after lunch, a window flew open and the headmaster called out, 'I told you to take your shoes off.'

'But, Sir, it's raining. I'll catch a cold,' I protested, incredulous at the need for me to say this.

'Never mind. If you won't do as you're told, you can pack your bags this evening,' he answered.

For the remainder of the day I went about in wet socks, allowed to put my shoes on only in time for evening prayers.

That night I rang my father. I used the telephone in a dormitory-house that was supervised by a fine teacher, Brother Bernard Cummins, whom I admired for his ability to convey how exciting the life of the mind could be. I asked my father to collect me the next morning and told him that I didn't want to stay another day in the school. He implored me to say for the duration of the year, pleading so anxiously that I agreed to consider it. I must have been shouting hysterically, for when I stepped outside the booth, Brother Cummins called me to his room. There he comforted me and urged me to heed my father's pleas.

I did so and stayed the year by which time my father had completely forgotten the incident. He was therefore shocked when I told him that I had done as he asked, and that I now intended to go to school in Melbourne. Unknown to him, I had been accepted into Melbourne High School, then one of the finest schools in the state, thanks to the intervention of a kind woman, Mrs Creath Caldwell. A speech teacher in Melbourne, she had heard me at a public-speaking competition. She wrote congratulating me and welcomed me to her home if I were visiting Melbourne. I replied telling her I intended to study in Melbourne the following year and asked which schools she recommended. She had a son at Melbourne High School and arranged an interview. I sat the entrance exam and was accepted.

My father refused to allow me to go. He said that I had started at St Patrick's and so should finish, that I would go to ruin, a boy of sixteen alone in Melbourne, living in boarding houses. I told him that I wasn't seeking his permission, that I intended to go, and that the only question was whether he would support me. We fought angrily, but I was determined and when finally he realised this and that he could not stop me, he agreed to pay my board and whatever else I needed. For years, however, he insisted I had made the wrong decision, not because any of his predictions came true, but only because I had not finished what I had started. Some years later when I changed from psychology to philosophy at university, he took the same attitude. He thought it a weakness in me.

In Melbourne, I lived for a time in a series of rooming houses, but eventually took a room at the house where Hora was boarding. It was owned by the same people from whom he had rented in Prahran—friends of his and my father's. Hora had a room and a small kitchen in which we often sat talking. He had a routine each evening, of making a cup of weak black tea, cutting a small slice of often dry bread, and two or three centimetres of salami. He cut the bread and sausage into pieces no bigger than a fingernail and slowly ate them while sipping his tea. The frugality and ritual would have impressed Mahatma Gandhi.

It was during this period, which lasted until halfway into my first year at university, that I had my only adult quarrel with Hora. At university I became attracted to radical left-wing politics. When I had talked about this with him, I noticed he was reticent and disapproving. I had a guitar and a book of protest songs. One evening I sang a song about strike-breakers with these words: 'The scabs crawl in, the scabs crawl out, the scabs crawl under and all about.'

Hora lost his temper. 'Don't you know that most unions are infiltrated by communists? Don't you know how ruthless they are? Don't you know what butchers they have been? Is this what a university education does for you?'

For more than a month he did not speak to me, though I often went to his kitchen hoping that he would.

At first I thought that Hora's anger had turned cold,

that he had simply turned his back on me, and I was very hurt. I was mistaken. He knew that I knew how many millions had perished under communism, for he had often told me. Given that I knew, how could I not care? But how could I claim to care if I treated it all so lightly? If I was now such a morally shallow person, what could he say to me? How could he speak to me of anything that mattered?

These questions cut into his heart, for he loved me. For him the pleasure of talking even about trivial matters depended on his knowing that the person with whom he was speaking was one whose responses to other topics could be trusted to be serious and decent. That was essential to his joy in conversation. Hora did not refuse to speak to me out of anger or indignation. He simply couldn't speak. I became, quite literally, some-one to whom he had nothing to say. This happened more than once in his life with other people. When he spoke to me again he did not mention the incident and, when I moved elsewhere, we saw each other often.

chapter eleven

My father told the story that one evening he prayed to God to give him a good wife if he was deserving of one. A few days later he went to Melbourne and asked friends if they knew of a woman who wanted to marry. It happened that they had heard of a Yugoslav divorcee who worked in a factory in Yarraville. A meeting was arranged and that is how he first met Milka.

She was twenty-nine and, as he put it, 'just right, not too tall, not too short, not too fat, not too thin, not too dark, not too light'. In fact, she was very attractive, in appearance and in personality. She told him that she couldn't cook, to which he replied that it didn't matter provided she did it and the washing. To his embarrassment he realised at their first meeting that he had virtually no money with him, so he borrowed from her to take her to dinner. They met again in Melbourne a few weeks later. She had her hair permed and coloured and, although he told her it made her 'look like a monkey', it did not stop her from coming to live in Maryborough, in September 1963 on the night before Tom Lillie's funeral.

They agreed to live together for a trial period. It was not easy for Milka. At close quarters my father was still unmistakably ill. This might excuse his behaviour, but it did not make living with him any easier. For one thing, the need to make allowances often frustrated the natural development and expression of her anger. For another, she found the acknowledgment that she was living with someone who was mentally ill more disturbing, even frightening, than the thought that she had married someone of bad or unpredictable character.

They often fought, sometimes vigorously and physically, although Milka seemed in these stoushes to give as good as she got. I sometimes separated them, declaring in the fatuous tone of a teenager who believed himself to be sophisticated that they should show more 'maturity'. The house shook with their battles, which almost always ended with Milka threatening to leave. My father said that she was free to go, but only in the morning, after they had slept the night together. I don't think that she ever went.

I am sure that is because she recognised him to be a good and unusual man. Throughout their marriage she was financially independent, always taking half of what they earned together. She went wherever she wanted by herself, knowing that infidelity would lead to divorce. Although he had insisted that she cook, he really meant unless he was not inclined to, which he often was. The division he knew from his childhood, between women's and men's work, played little role in his life. He sewed, cooked and baked, teaching Milka how to make strudel with their own pastry (thin as a cigarette paper), doughnuts and other things. His respect for her independence was unusual in husbands of his vintage from their part of Europe and Milka knew it. They married six months after she first came to Maryborough.

Soon afterwards they began to build a workshop on land my father had bought on the industrial side of Maryborough. When Tom Lillie died, his daughter asked my father to leave the blacksmith shop because she intended to lease the farm. Milka and he built the workshop together, digging the foundations, laying the cement, erecting the building. He made the steel frame, the supporting stanchions and the large steel supports for the roof which he put in place with only Milka to help him. When it was built Milka worked with him, grinding the welding residues and helping him with the painting by bringing and taking away garden settings. She did this for many hundreds of garden settings over the years.

She was constantly with him, usually working until evening, and then she often stayed with him in the workshop until 10 or 11 p.m., preferring to be there than home alone. He made an iron stove so that she would be warm in winter, especially in the evenings, and was proud of the fact that it warmed the entire large workshop within half an hour, glowing red hot. When the garden settings were finished he hired a semi-trailer to take them to Melbourne where he painted them because he did not want any to arrive with chipped paintwork. He often stayed in a caravan park and sometimes with his uncle. Every evening he telephoned Milka who was impatient for his call and for his return.

This was the uncle from whom he fled when he was thirteen. During the fifties, my father sent him expensive medicines which kept him alive and later brought him and his son to Australia. He received little thanks for it, not from his uncle who threw him out of his house in Melbourne, nor from many others whom he helped bring to Australia and in other ways.

Compassion went unusually deep in my father. It showed itself all his life in the help he gave those in need and in the pain he visibly felt for their pain. He was literally incapable of not helping someone genuinely in need if he had the means to do so. Whenever he made money, through his business or later when he sold the land and the workshop, he looked to see who needed some. He could no more have money without giving some to others who needed it than he could eat steak and not give some to his dogs.

He was like that from the time he was a boy. Over the years he sent thousands of dollars to relatives in Yugoslavia. When he sold his workshop he immediately offered Hora six thousand dollars to pay off a bank debt. Hora refused the offer. My father persisted. Why should he have money sitting in the bank when Hora was in debt and paying interest? Always Hora refused, but he was joyful to know that he had such a friend.

More often than not my father's generosity was abused, and although it pained him it did not diminish his impulse to give. Once he paid the airfares for an entire family: husband, wife and three children. In those days—the mid-sixties—this cost almost as much as a modest house such as his in Maryborough. The husband had assured my father that he would repay him as soon as he was able, but when he arrived, and was actually living with his family in my father's house, he pointed out that there existed no written agreement concerning repayments. Notwithstanding this, my father allowed him to stay, but his patience broke when, a month or so into their stay, he produced a three-quarters-full bottle of *slivovitz* as a present for my father. Incredulous that the man could not even give him a full bottle and unable to bear this added insult to his substantial injury, my father asked him to speed up his search for a house.

He left, but lived for some years in Maryborough where he worked hard, bought a house and a new car yet offered my father not a cent in repayment. Instead, he came to the house to show off his new car, condescending to my father because he still drove an old Holden. My father's and Milka's relatives in Yugoslavia were no better. They often wrote pleading for money, often pretending to be ill, but when he and Milka went to visit them they discovered that the money they had sent for medicine and other necessities had contributed to the renovation of houses that were larger and better furnished than his. On one occasion when Milka was there, one of them actually asked for, and was given, the coat from her back.

Extreme though these examples are, they are true to the outlook of most of my father's Yugoslav relatives. They were somewhat redeemed by the fact that they worked so hard, often at two jobs, laying the bricks for their own houses or working as labourers to the brick-layers. This was before it became fashionable—mostly for a later generation of people living in Australia—to make money defrauding the social services, feigning work injuries, wearing neck braces and walking on crutches, but abandoning them when they moved heavy furniture in the privacy of their homes. Some of his relatives were also overtaken by religion, converting from their Orthodox faith to become evangelical Baptists and urging my father to do the same. There was an epidemic of such conversions.

My father found these conversions amusing and irri-tating: amusing at a distance, irritating when his relatives came to his house and sang hymns instead of conversing. They had so little understanding of my father, and so little understanding of themselves, that they did not realise that he would never be converted by people whom he regarded as hypocrites. His sense of religion and their desire for wealth and prestige were radically incompatible. He believed that those who were gen-uinely religious felt no need to distinguish themselves from others in such ways.

Not that there was a chance of anyone converting him. He looked with suspicion on those who changed their religion, whatever it was and for whatever reason. He prayed each day to a God he believed would listen to all prayers that came from a pure heart. He thought it absurd to believe that God would listen only to the prayers of those who belonged to particular institutions, as absurd as believing that He would listen to prayers in only one language.

My father's religion, as it was most deeply lived by him, was quite separate from the superstitions that tormented him during his illness and which later became a settled part of his outlook. If his superstitions had mattered to him religiously, if they had seriously informed the spiritual dimensions of his life, then he would have set them polemically against the speculative beliefs of other religions. But he always regarded such beliefs as inessential to what he understood as genuine religiosity. He had no interest in doctrine. At the centre of his religious sensibility was the idea of a pure heart responsive to those in need. Of itself, that idea did not make him religious. What made him religious was the connection of that idea with prayer rather than with his spiritualist beliefs.

His spiritualism—as distinct from his profound spirituality—was superficial and unreligious, a belief in spirits floating free of the body, in sleep and after death, travelling to other planets. He talked often about this, but apart from when he was ill and alarmed by his beliefs in the malign intentions of these spirits, he always propounded his views in the mood of what he called 'just talking'—speculation—and they had no connection with his moral conduct.

His belief in an afterlife was unconnected with his sense of good and evil, reward and punishment or any conception of the last judgment. But when he talked seriously about religion, as for example when he begged me to pray, dismayed that I could not, I did not feel that he was urging me to adopt a supernatural means to a natural or even a supernatural end. Rather, his sense of our deep need of prayer was the expression of his belief that only a life of prayer could enable one to consent to great and protracted misfortune and for that consent to go sufficiently deep to save one from despair. I believe that is why the only time that his spiritualism connected with anything deep in his life was when it intersected with his fatalism. The God he prayed to was the God whom he encountered in the Bible stories of his childhood which came mostly from the Old Testament—the God of Abraham, Isaac, Jacob and Job.

Despite judging most of his relatives to be crooks and hypocrites, untruthful in their words and deeds, greedy in their pursuits while preaching the puritanical gospel of the Baptists, he enjoyed their company when they could keep off talking about religion. He longed for European society, saying that he felt like 'a prisoner' in Australia. He meant that, although he had good neighbours, in Maryborough he had almost no one with whom he could enjoy the generous and open forms of conviviality that characterised European hospitality as he knew it. He complained that one could not just drop in on Australians and talk freely for hours; one had, as he put it, always to 'make an appointment'. Whereas if you went into a European home, you would generally be offered food and talk, both in generous quantities. He especially missed Hora, but Hora had married in the mid-sixties and was preoccupied with domestic life and especially with his two young children, Irena and Raymond.

My father loved to be among people, a fact that made his years alone at Baringhup so very hard. He enjoyed going to Melbourne, especially to the Victoria Market where he savoured the bustle. If there were so many people that you had always to rub shoulders, then so much the better. He would talk for hours to various stallholders.

To escape his 'prison' he talked of returning to Yugoslavia when the communist regime collapsed. In 1981 he went, but on his return to Australia he complained about the rudeness, verging on brutality, of many of the people and their actual lack of concern for their neighbours despite their readiness to talk and to put food and *slivovitz* on the table for visitors. He thought services were appalling and spent a miserable night waiting to be attended in a hospital in which patients lay on sheets smeared with other people's faeces. His experience of Yugoslavia gave him a renewed appreciation of life in Australia, but he still longed, and longed all his life, for the European conviviality he knew as a young man, even in Germany, and with his friends and relatives in Melbourne.

During the sixties and early seventies, my father more or less recovered from his illness, but he was permanently changed by it. He never again troubled about his dress. During the week he wore only his overalls and generally would shave only once a week, on weekends. His face had long ago lost its youthful softness and as it reflected his character accurately he became even more handsome. As always, he wore his cut-down slipper-shoes. His detestation of superficialities extended not only to his appearances, but also to decorations and furnishings in the house.

This was a kind of puritanism, but it was not, as puritanism often is, small-minded or mean-spirited. I believe this was because his sense of what mattered did not come from conversion to a doctrine of any sort. All his life he had a strong sense of moral reality and with it a belief in the connection between goodness and simplicity. These became austere when he confronted despair and terror in his madness.

People argue about whether suffering ennobles. There is another and different thought, which is that only suffering makes one wise. Of course, people can suffer the most horrific experiences and emerge even more superficial than they were before. Some kinds of wisdom, however—the kinds that show themselves not only in thoughts, but in the integrity of an authoritatively lived life—are given only to those who have suffered deep and long. His affliction gave authority to much of what my father said, gave power to his language, rich in peasant imagery, and spared his harsh moral judgment from any tinge of moralism in the pejorative sense of that term which implies an ever-present readiness to point the finger at others and to turn one's back on them.

In one way, my father was a fierce moralist. Not about the big and controversial issues of the day, but about simple moral requirements such as honesty and concern for one's neighbour. If he thought you were a liar or a cheat or had acted unkindly, then he would say so to you without a trace of euphemism. But there was never anything in his judgment which implied you should be shunned by decent people. Though fierce and uncompromising, his judgments were not what we now call 'judgmental'.

Even his most severe judgments were made in many tones. If he called you an incorrigible liar he might do it angrily, scathingly, sorrowfully or, strange as it might sound, matter-of-factly, but never in a tone that suggested he would turn his back on you. You were always welcome at his table, to eat and more importantly to talk; always to talk. But he believed that it was essential to decent conversation that one not pretend to virtues one did not possess—as essential as being truthful about one's identity. Only then could conversation be true to its deeper potentialities and do its humanising work of opening up the possibilities of authentic human disclosure.

Not that my father's conversations were always intense. He enjoyed talking about anything that would not of itself—because of its deceit or meanness—foreclose the possibilities of something more serious. He regarded talk of business matters as properly restricted to working days, and for a time he prohibited it in his home on Sundays. He enjoyed gossip and would talk about anything that engaged with the ordinary dramas and follies of life in its variety. The ingenuity that had fuelled his paranoia also informed his wit, which was often mischievous and nourished by natural imagery.

He became a familiar figure in Maryborough, but few people would have seen him shaven or wearing anything other than overalls. He had little respect for the town's luminaries—the doctors, solicitors, businessmen or councillors. The council especially provoked his scornful anger because he saw in so many of its actions the vices he most detested: dishonesty and arrogant self-importance. On one occasion he went to the council chambers with his chainsaw and banged it on the bench declaring that he might cut off the heads of all the councillors, with one exception. He achieved his purpose which was to persuade the council to rescind an order demanding he remove his goats from the vacant block of land he had bought to build the house for Lydia. They knew he was only half joking. Their nervousness over his intentions was probably increased by the fact that a horror film, *Texas Chainsaw Massacre*, was popular at the time.

Often the unhappy people who were at the receiving end of his lashings struck me as torn between two responses. They were tempted to condescend to this foreigner, in his overalls, unshaven and speaking a broken English. But the intensity of his eyes, the sheer integrity of his demeanour, and the unquestionable authority of a man whose history and reputation they knew, would not allow them to do so. The simplicity of his moral convictions, that you not tell lies, that you not take money for shabby goods, that you not try to cover up a shoddy job, allowed for no controversy, and they knew these values were embodied in his life and work. Sometimes, to be confronted by him was like being confronted by a Biblical prophet, someone whose fierce purity made him transparent to the reality of the values he professed.

The impressiveness of his character was largely a consequence of its transformation by the terrors of his illness which left him with no patience for superficialities. His sense of what was superficial, however, was far from incontestable. He would have found incomprehensible Oscar Wilde's remark that only shallow people fail to be impressed by appearances. Wilde meant that much of what we call the surface of things in fact goes deep. Though my father had made many beautiful objects, his pleasure in being able to make them was curiously detached from an appreciation of their beauty. His interest in beautiful things others had made lacked almost entirely an aesthetic component. He was interested in the craftsmanship, but not in the beauty achieved by it. My father had no real sense of how beauty in architecture, artefacts, manners, speech or style of eating, for example, could grace our lives. He associated concern for these things with a desire for prestige, a desire to set oneself apart and look down on others. He came across many examples of such concern for status, but he was unable to see beyond them to what they corrupted.

By the same token, I doubt that Wilde would have understood my father or appreciated his virtues. And it is doubtful that my father could have been as impressive as he was if he had appreciated Wilde's point. One can appreciate both in thought, but I doubt that both can be lived with the kind of integrity with which my father lived his values. The cost of living one of them fully, authentically and passionately, is either ignorance or repression. My father's Old Testament integrity was partly a function of his blindness.

As a young man it was hard for me to understand that fact and my failure to do so, together with those aspects of my father's illness that tried everyone's patience, sometimes caused us to quarrel. His character and illness and my youth occasionally combined explosively. The ferocity of his temper ignited mine. Once he hit me, knocking me to the floor. I rose in a blind rage and went for him. Milka intercepted me and when I pushed her aside she fell against the hot stove. I came to my senses when I saw what I had done to her.

My father and I were both shaken by this episode. He told me that if we could not agree, then perhaps we should not see each other, but we should part amicably. I thought about it, but then realised it was an absurd proposition. I loved him too deeply and knew that after what we had shared at Frogmore, no quarrel could estrange us. I sometimes cursed this realisation for it had the effect of frustrating the natural development of my anger to a point where I would at least contemplate not seeing him again.

On one occasion, when I came home for Christmas, we quarrelled within minutes of my arrival. I drove back to Melbourne at such speed that my car became airborne when I hit a level crossing. When I reached Melbourne I realised that I must either break with my father or return to Maryborough, it being a serious matter for me to refuse to come for Christmas. I ruled out the former, so I drove back, again at high speed in order to get there before midnight. When I arrived my father asked where I had been. I told him that I had been to Melbourne. Incredulous that I could have been to Melbourne and back in such a short time, he berated me for driving like a lunatic. If I had not bitten my tongue and said nothing we would have quarrelled and I would have driven back to Melbourne again.

My father's strength of character had much to do with his recovery, but it could not have been only due to that. Stability in character goes hand-in-hand with a capacity for steady judgment which insanity undermines. The terror of insanity lies mainly in the fact that one cannot overcome or even properly confront it through any direct application of thought and will, and so one feels desperately helpless. Often the will can only be exercised indirectly, supported by medicines or by psychotherapy, but the resolve to persist in these supports is itself constantly undermined. And often one cannot rely on one's mind because that too has been at least partially lost to the illness. My father recognised this when he said, 'There is no sickness worse than mental sickness.'

In his defence of the content of his paranoid fantasies and of their reality, my father displayed great ingenuity, and I knew that there was no point in trying to reason with him, for he was not in any ordinary sense merely or even radically mistaken. He was out of touch with reality in a way that defied rational or factual correction, by himself or by others, and the intermittent realisation of that terrified him. To help him through his illness his strength of character needed the right kind of nurturing to function, and that, I believe, was given to him by the relative stability of his life with Milka.

It mattered to that stability that she and I got on as well as we did. My father often remarked on it and it gratified him greatly. Even though he knew I had shown no hostility to Lydia or later to her mother, he feared that once he actually lived as man and wife with another woman I would resent her just on account of that. He was quite mistaken for I warmed to Milka more or less from the first day she arrived. She had a girlish innocence and a vivacity that charmed many who met her. But mostly I was impressed by how she bore my father's illness and how hard she worked with him.

She was always open and affectionate with me, without ever pressing her claims as a stepmother, and was grateful for whatever acknowledgment I accorded her in this regard. Generous to me and my friends, she always welcomed me and them, glad of our presence in the house. I thought my father immensely lucky to have her, and often thought he was foolish in his insensitivity to her desire for small luxuries in the house and that he should dress a little more respectably. When she went on her first trip to Yugoslavia, I was worried that she would not return.

It grieved them that they could not have children. When it became clear that it was impossible for Milka to conceive, they sought to adopt a child. They were refused on the grounds of age, but I assume that it had as much to do with my father's history of mental illness. It was an understandable refusal, but a regrettable one. He loved children and would have made a fine father to them, as he had been to me. His pleasure in them was an expression of his love of all living things and their regeneration. When my former wife, Margaret, met him for the first time, his words to her after greeting her were, 'Look out the window. The cats have kittens and the dogs have pups. The goats have kids and the hens have chickens. Everything breeds around here except my son.'

chapter twelve

'No. He's the philosopher,' said my father, pointing to me. 'I'm an astronomer.'

He went on to explain that while he studied the heavens, I had no talent for it. It was late at night in the mid-eighties and he was entertaining, in the kitchen of his home in Maryborough, four or five middle-aged hippies who lived in the old Catholic church in Carisbrook, eight kilometres from Maryborough. One of them had remarked that my father and I were related as senior and junior philosophers. He was a relatively serious painter while the others sought alternative ways of living. They thought my father lived, to some degree, the life they aspired to and they enjoyed his conversation whose style and content they assimilated to their rebellion against more conventional ways of living. Mistakenly, they took him for a kindred spirit.

My father met them after his cows broke into their property and ate their sapling fruit trees. He built them chicken-wire cages and for this they allowed him to graze his cows on their land during a drought. They responded to my father with the delighted double-mindedness with which some Australians discovered multiculturalism They responded to his charisma, admired his skills and his peasant know-how, but their tone of voice and the ease with which they touched him and comported themselves in his home betrayed the qualification that it was, after all, *peasant* know-how. They were also intemperately fond of his homemade *slivovitz*.

His remark about philosophers and astronomers, and the circumstances in which he made it, showed two important things about this stage of his life. He still studied the moon, the stars and the clouds, looking for patterns that would reveal meaning to him. But the light-hearted way he referred to his superstitions revealed that they no longer tormented him even though they often furnished the basis for predictions of serious events, such as someone's illness or death. His firm belief that he could predict events did not engage seriously with his feelings, except insofar as he often felt it to be a curse. What went deep with him was his response when the events he predicted came to pass, his pained fatalistic acceptance of them rather than the fact that he predicted them.

The circumstances of his remarks were also an indication of his changed status in the community, partly because of the respect accorded to his strength of character, and partly because attitudes to New Australians had changed. That change had many dimensions and was, as I have remarked, not always free from condescension in the very people who sang its praises. My father noted this, but he and Milka were nonetheless glad of the change, recognising its generosity, and the same distinctively Australian decency that he had known in many of the people he met when he lived at Frogmore.

By now my father had retired from his ironwork. He spent most of his time in his vegetable garden, or on his land outside Carisbrook, caring for his animals. He was slightly diminished by his retirement. His demeanour was less self-assured, almost imperceptibly so, but sufficiently to allow the hippies from Carisbrook to feel free with him in their manners, and physically to touch him, in ways that struck him and me as insolent. Only two years before they would not have dared.

He was a superb worker but never a good businessman, so he became increasingly vulnerable to the shabby and often ruthless business practices which became notorious in the eighties. Most things became more expensive at the same time that their quality declined. He complained that steel was too often not properly tempered and that the quality of tools had declined while their price had risen. Shoddy workmanship or manufacturing angered him but he was particularly dismayed at the difficulty he had in getting anyone to accept responsibility for it. Although his pleasure in his work was undiminished, he became increasingly disillusioned with business and eventually gave it up.

Even before he did this, he and Milka had many animals. For a time they had twenty or so cows which Milka hoped would produce profitable calves, but they bought them at the beginning of a severe drought in the early eighties and, after spending many months cutting hay, they sold them. After they paid for the truck to take the cows to market in Castlemaine, they had enough profit to buy a carton of cigarettes. It was a heartbreaking time, when farmers shot their sheep and cattle in large pits because they could not feed them and because they would incur substantial losses if they paid their transport to market.

When they had rid themselves of the burden of their cows, they turned their energies to cutting grass for their goats. My father and Milka sometimes went to Castlemaine market, and there they saw a goat with a broken leg. They took pity on it and brought it home to care for it. When the goat recovered, my father again felt sorry for it, believing it to be lonely, and therefore bought it a mate. That is how it started. Soon he and Milka had thirty goats from whom they received no material benefit. Occasionally my father killed one and ate it, and he milked some, but he almost always gave the milk to the dogs. The goats were often ill and vet fees took a sizeable portion of his and Milka's small income. When the drought came, my father knew the goats would starve unless he could get hay for them. He could not afford to buy the quantities he needed, so with a scythe and with Milka to help load the trailer he cut it himself.

He cut grass on the roadside, clearing the area between the roads and the fences literally for miles. In the summer sun, the work was exhausting and dangerous because of snakes which my father killed in large numbers over the years. He cut and then, with Milka, loaded the trailer, day after day, week after week. A farmer in the area told me, 'I can work. I know it. But nothing like that.' Alone one day, my father collapsed with pain in his chest and along his left arm. When he regained consciousness he went to the Maryborough hospital where he was told he was dehydrated. He said that the doctor who examined him did not even check his heart.

The attitude he expressed to the lone goat was the same that he showed to many animals. When he saw one he was inclined to think there should be two and, if the two did not make three or more, he fretted over them. The long backyard in Maryborough was often home to sick or breeding animals or to their offspring— baby goats, rabbits, chickens, ducks, turkeys, and of course pups and kittens. To the delight of my children there was sometimes a sick animal, usually a baby goat, in the kitchen where it could warm itself by the stove.

His compassion extended undiminished to his bees. On an occasion when we were repairing my car at night, the bees flew to where we were working, attracted to the light. A dozen or so were crushed between our hands and the engine block. My father became increasingly distressed as the number of dead bees increased. I had at least half a dozen stings, and felt ill because of them, but his sorrow was directed at the bees.

On winter mornings he gathered the bees which had not entered the hive the previous night, to all appearances quite dead as they lay on the grass. He took them into the kitchen, lay them on their backs on the table and held an electric light bulb about fifteen centimetres above them, moving it continuously so that they would not be harmed by a concentration of heat. It was an entrancing and moving experience to see their legs twitch, so slightly at first that one wondered whether it had really happened, and then more surely. After a few minutes they turned themselves right way up, still unsteady on their feet. When they looked ready to fly we took them outside.

Jack did not move to Maryborough with us. My father knew that he could not let him roam free there: his destructive ways would soon see him shot. Rather than cage him my father left him at Frogmore, hoping that he would fly off with a passing flock of cockatoos, his wing having grown again. My father's dogs assumed the place previously taken by Jack in his affections. They spent the day with him and, in the evenings, when Milka was not with him, they lay on the bed with her while she watched television.

My father fed them whatever he ate partly because he could see no reason why dogs should be denied a varied diet, but mostly because he believed that it was mean-spirited to deny them food merely because it was expensive or supposedly too good for dogs. He sometimes offended people who brought him continental cakes or sausages from Melbourne, because he always gave some to the dogs who he believed should share the treat. He took the dogs to the drive-in movies, convinced that they enjoyed them, and from behind it was indeed a strange sight to see the heads of two dogs who were sitting on the back seat apparently attentive to the screen.

My father's behaviour to his animals struck some people as sentimental. Some said that he treated his dogs as though they were human beings. They were quite wrong, for his practice always expressed a wisely judged sense of the radical difference in kind between human beings and animals, even though he sometimes blurred that distinction in conversation. When his dogs died, he was heartbroken and cried. He told me that sometimes the pain in his chest lasted for weeks and tears would catch him without warning. Even so, he merely buried them in a hole in the backyard and would have thought it absurd to observe any of the rituals we think appropriate when human beings die. Sometimes, to explain his generous treatment of his dogs, he would say that if dogs go to heaven, and he met them there, he hoped that they would say that he treated them well. I always thought that to be a beautiful sentiment, beautifully expressed.

Not all injured animals fared so well as his first goat. One day while visiting a farmer my father noticed a pig with a broken leg.

'This pig, what will you do with him?' he asked.

'Probably shoot him and throw him on the tip,' the farmer replied.

My father looked again at the pig and said, 'There's a lot of sausage in him.'

The farmer gave my father the pig, gratis. With some difficulty he managed to get it home, slaughtered it and indeed made sausage of it. Smoked and spicy, it tasted superb. I estimated that were you to buy it in Melbourne delicatessens, the lot would cost almost a thousand dollars. The next year he bought a pig at the market, again injured, for eighty dollars, and did the same with it. Such enterprise enabled him and Milka to live well on their meagre income.

When she was little, my younger daughter, Eva, was troubled by the fact that my father killed animals, even though she knew he killed them only to eat them. I asked her whether she knew of anyone, or had even read of anyone, who treated animals more kindly than her grandfather. She immediately replied that there was no one. In itself of course that was no argument, but argument was not needed to put an end to her unease. The authority of her grandfather's example taught her that there was no serious moral gap between his kindness to animals and his preparedness sometimes to kill them. She learned through his example what it might mean to kill an animal.

My father's sense of the difference between human

beings and animals was not always conventional. Once, when I visited him, he told me how his goats had been killed, their innards torn out and their carcasses left. Some people attributed the savage killings to a wild mountain lion which rumour said had been seen in the area. Mountain lions are not natural to any part of Australia and most people gave as much credence to this as they did to tales of the Loch Ness monster.

My father put the savage killings down to human cruelty. He had waited some nights hidden behind a log, hoping to catch the killers. Around ten at night, he took his rifle and asked me whether I was coming with him. I knew my father and so I knew that nothing I could say would deter him from going. He would either go alone or go with me. I was taken back to the time when we went to Sydney, he intent on shooting Lydia's husband. As I did then, I knew that because he had asked me it was morally impossible for me to refuse.

We sat behind a log at his property outside Caris-brook, on a crisp, moonless winter night, the sky black and opulent with stars. As we talked I wondered whether I could stop him if it came to a showdown, and whether the University of London would still employ me after I had been in a shoot-out on an Australian farm. Mercifully, no one came.

For a time after he stopped making garden settings my father kept the workshop, but made things only for locals—some garden settings, but mostly gates or verandah posts. Antiques and craftsmanship had become fashionable and I tried to convince him that there might be a market for beaten ironwork, but he had lost interest in the business world, and so stopped making things even for private sale. It was a pity, for the beaten ironwork of his youth in Germany, rather than the fashionable wrought-iron of the fifties, was the source of his deepest pride, and had he taken it up again he would have made things which were superbly crafted and of great beauty.

He and Milka lived on their pensions. For a time they were virtually self-sufficient, growing almost all their own vegetables, killing their meat, sometimes goats, mostly lambs, making their own jams and pickling conserves. He even grew his own tobacco from seeds brought from Yugoslavia and made cigars, but the tobacco needed so much pesticide to survive that smoking it made one sick. Like most Europeans of peasant stock he was a late convert to natural forms of pest control. Generations of them had suffered heartbreaking losses and therefore looked upon chemical pesticides as their saviour. For a long time many resisted natural pesticides with a ferocity that was fuelled by the pain of their past losses.

During this period, in the early and mid-eighties, my father urged me to try to find my adopted sisters.

He had done it many times since I was a teenager and he could not understand why I showed no interest in doing so. The truth is that I had no sense of extended family, not of my father's family nor of my mother's, until I met Maria, my mother's sister, who had helped look after me when I was a baby. Through a series of accidents I arrived unannounced on Maria's doorstep in Germany more than twenty years after she had last seen me. I was then twenty-seven years old. When she opened the door, I asked, 'Frau Becker?'

She look puzzled for only a second or two. 'Raimond! *Was für eine Überraschung!*' (What a surprise).

I fell in love with her straightaway, no doubt partly because she looked and sounded so like my mother. All day she said to herself, '*Was für eine Überraschung!*'

This new-found sense of family, my love for Maria and her children Ulrike and Andrea, gradually awakened in me a desire to find Susan and Barbara. The adoption laws had changed, making it possible for me to seek them out. It proved to be easy, for they had been adopted by a couple who had lived all their married life in the same house in Melbourne. When the social worker rang the couple telling them that I was looking for my sisters, they reluctantly informed Barbara and Susan of the fact. Neither knew they had a brother and were astonished and confused to learn of it. Barbara lived in Melbourne and Susan in Wodonga three hundred kilometres to the north. Both were now married with children. To the joy of my father and Hora we were reunited, nervously but happily, in the mid-eighties.

My father believed that for brother and sister not to know of each other's whereabouts, let alone existence, was so profoundly against the order of things that it constituted a metaphysical damage to their lives. When Barbara and Susan came with me to Maryborough, visited the graves of our mother and Mitru and sat in my father's kitchen and talked, he felt the damage had been repaired. He believed that whatever might happen in the future, nothing could compromise the intrinsic good of our having found each other. As well as anyone he knew that truth could be painful, but he denied that it could be harmful, believing that its capacity to do damage was dependent entirely on the attitude one took to it. He could not understand how anyone could prefer to live in ignorance or illusion about anything that mattered to the meaning of their lives. Hora was also inclined to this belief, but less strongly than my father.

He and my father were comforted by the fact that Susan and Barbara were married with children, taking it as a sign that the girls had not been so damaged by their childhood as to be incapable of living an ordinary life. Hora noted how Susan looked like his grandmother. My father noted that both girls had the long noses bequeathed by my mother's father to his family.

Although my father never admitted it, quitting his ironwork was not good for him. He had worked hard all his life and grew up in a culture which disposed him to see work in the light of the old biblical curse, a necessity to whose yoke one would consent only if one could not free oneself of it. He was puzzled by people who worked when they did not need to, suspecting their motives to be either greed or the need for status. This was despite the fact that he enjoyed his ironwork and found such fulfilment in it, and also despite the fact that he and Hora were inclined to believe that depth and real contentment were to be found only in a life governed by necessity. Wisdom, they believed, lay in consent to that necessity. Superficiality and restlessness were in store for those who fled it.

But my father did not integrate this wisdom into his life. After he sold his workshop he was incapable of not working and incapable of fully understanding that fact. So he created necessities for himself: the animals which he *had* to feed and the garden which he *had* to tend. But apart from the periods of drought when he cut grass, working as hard as few men could, his animals and garden did not give him enough to do under the mantle of necessity, and he began to decline.

Without real work he again became vulnerable to depression and tended to brood on his moral disappointment with the world. He longed for visitors who seldom came, the distance from Melbourne being too great. He was especially glad to see Hora, but Hora now suffered terribly from arthritis and found it difficult to drive. Even when he came with me, he was reluctant to do so in winter, for Maryborough was colder than Melbourne and the unheated bedroom was painful for him. A bitterness, which I had never seen in him before, entered my father's life. The pain of it showed in his eyes.

His sorrow was deepened by the fact that I lived in England. He often said that it did not matter, since I was with him every day in his heart. He reasoned that because I was born of European parents I would discover my European roots when I went to England and he predicted that I would not return, even though I went intending to stay only for as long as it took to do a PhD. At the airport he reminded me that he had left Yugoslavia never to return. As I left he sang 'Waltzing Matilda'.

Nonetheless I knew that he wished for me to return. He could not understand that I wanted to stay there for my work, partly because he did not understand my commitment to the life of the mind. It troubled him because he saw in it a sign of the restlessness that he feared would be a legacy of my childhood. His anxiety over this, rather than the more common desire of parents to want material benefits for their children, made him wish that I could live an uncomplicated life in Melbourne working as a solicitor or doctor, resting well on weekends and visiting him at least once a month. He took some pride in my successes, but his attitude to them is conveyed in what he said when he saw a doll's house I had made for my children. It had a carved stairway and carved mantelpieces, corniced ceilings, panelled doors, electric lights and power points. After inspecting it he expressed his admiration, adding, 'I see that you have some brains after all.'

Milka felt their growing isolation as much as my father, and both complained of it. My father was partly responsible for it because he sometimes alienated potential visitors by his reprimands when they did not come after they had expressed an intention to do so. He reprimanded them because his moral outlook could not tolerate a significant distinction between a promise and the declaration of an intention.

If you said that you would come on this or that day, even though the context would have made it clear to anyone else that this was no promise, merely the declaration of your intention, he would hold you to it as though you had promised, and would sometimes call you a liar if you did not come. This was not mere cantankerousness but, as with his inability to understand self-deception, a conceptual matter. His failure to distinguish statements of intentions from promises was the expression of a perspective that treated the difference as of no moral significance.

Because the verbal expression of an intention may often be the same as the verbal expression of a promise, sometimes only context or tone enables people to distinguish one from the other. My father's profound regard for the spoken word was of a kind that sometimes made him literal-minded and tone-deaf to context. If you defended yourself against the accusation that you had broken your word, he became impatient, treating the defence as an expression of bad faith, a failure of character, a refusal to be true to the words you had spoken. If you said that you hoped to come, or that you might come, that was fine. If you said that you would come, he would hold you to it under pain of lack of integrity, of a failure to have your character integrated by a commitment to your words. He seemed to believe that only a self in that way integrated had risen to the humanising potential of speech. I think that is why he ran together, so literally, the words one spoke and the giving of one's word.

His decline was hastened by heart disease, which accelerated rapidly soon after he first developed the symptoms of angina. Within a couple of years he was barely able to walk. At first he said that he would refuse all operations because, as he put it, he would not consent to be 'cut up'. He meant that he would not prolong his life with many operations because it was unnatural and undignified to flee death when nature had intended it for you, an indignity compounded by going to your grave mutilated by operations whose scars testified to your vain desire to live beyond your appointed time. His attitude was shaped by the fate of cancer patients.

When he realised that the bypass he needed would be a once-only operation, he reluctantly agreed to it. My difficulty in persuading him was increased by his doctor who convinced him that he was not in urgent need of an operation. When my father arrived at St Vincent's Hospital in Melbourne for his angiogram, the doctor who tested him was shocked that his condition had been allowed to deteriorate so far.

I was in London at the time of his operation—a triple bypass. My wife, Yael, came every day to visit him. Immediately after the operation, when he was in the recovery room, she became anxious because he was unconscious for a long time. She alerted an attendant who agreed there was cause for concern and suggested that my father may have suffered a stroke. He urged her to call his name. Again and again she called, 'Romulus', but he did not respond. Hours after she had gone, he emerged from deep unconsciousness. The operation was a success, but he had suffered a stroke during the angiogram and another during the operation, which left him paralysed along one side and unable to remember anything, not even why he was in hospital.

Later Yael came each evening to massage him, so that he might regain control of his arms and legs, to rub his back with methylated spirits so that he would not get sores, and to comfort and encourage him. She was then teaching five days a week, working a stall at the Victoria Market at weekends and looking after Dahlia and Michelle, her two small children whom she often took with her to the hospital. My father was grateful and also glad of visitors, but Yael noticed how he hoped every visitor was Milka, his disappointment when she did not come and how his eyes lit up when she did. He kissed her on the lips like a young man would. Most of the time Milka stayed in Maryborough because the animals needed looking after. My father would not countenance their neglect for his sake, but it became evident how profound his need of Milka was.

He recovered quite quickly from his strokes, but never fully regained the control of his left hand. With great difficulty he gave up smoking, but he drew the line at continental sausages or smoked bacon which he enjoyed until his death. A year after the bypass, he had another angiogram. Neither his specialist nor his local doctor told those who were to perform it that he had suffered a stroke during the previous one. He had another stroke and lost most of the sight in his left eye. No apologies came from the doctors. Working in the garden was all that he was now capable of because he could not weld or even hold middle-sized tools. Nor could he drive. He often looked at his hands and wondered what had become of him.

'Can you believe how I used to be?' he asked me. 'I'm good for nothing. Just for the rubbish heap.'

chapter thirteen

On a Monday morning in May 1996 my father complained to Milka of pain in his stomach which became severe during the course of the afternoon. He went to the doctor who told him he had the flu. During the night the pain had become unbearable. On Tuesday morning it was so severe that he could not write a greeting in a birthday card that Milka was writing for me, even though it was for my fiftieth birthday. That afternoon she rang the doctor, very worried, asking whether mere flu could cause such terrible pain. She was assured it could.

The next day, Wednesday, his condition even worse, she took my father to the clinic. His doctor was away, so she went to another, who gruffly told him to take off his trousers and to climb onto the examining bed. Milka protested at this brutish treatment, pointing out that my father's pain was so severe that he could barely stand. She refused to accept any suggestion that my father needed anything less than hospitalisation. That afternoon he was taken by ambulance to the hospital in Ballarat.

Milka phoned me that Wednesday night around ten. I was preparing to leave for Tasmania where I was to give some lectures, to be joined by Yael at the weekend. Because my father knew that we were in need of a holiday, he told Milka to say nothing to me in case I should cancel my trip. Fortunately she finally disregarded this instruction. I phoned the Ballarat hospital to be told that the doctors had not settled on a diagnosis. An hour later they conducted an exploratory operation and telephoned me just after midnight to inform me of the result. My father had a dead gut, caused by a clot in the artery supplying his stomach. They thought it unlikely that he would live for more than twenty-four hours.

I decided not to phone Milka because I hoped that

she was asleep. I knew she would need all her strength over the coming days. I phoned Hora, told him what the doctors had told me, and asked if he wanted to come with me to Ballarat, first thing in the morning. Of course he did. Milka phoned an hour later and I told her the news.

In the morning, Hora and I drove first to Maryborough to collect Milka and then on to Ballarat. The doctors in intensive care had told my father what was wrong with him and that there was no hope. He was barely conscious, partly because of the anaesthetic, and partly because his entire system was poisoned because his gut no longer functioned. He made a whimpering sound at the expulsion of each breath. I thought he was frightened because he knew that he was dying, but was unable to muster sufficient consciousness even to try to come to terms with the fact. Hora thought that he was probably assailed by terrible imagery, a consequence of his poisoned system and his incapacity to regain full consciousness.

He remained in that state throughout the day, able sometimes to hear, but seldom to respond with more than one word.

'Are you in pain?' I asked him many times.

'No,' he replied each time.

The surgeon advised that my father would not be discomfited if he did not have the oxygen mask, so we removed it because it covered much of his face, obscuring what little expressiveness remained to him. In these last hours, I wanted him to be as fully present to us as was possible.

Milka and Hora went home to Maryborough around six. As he left, Hora called, 'Gaita.' There was no response. Again he called, 'Gaita,' and then, 'Goodbye.' His voice broke and his entire body heaved as he said goodbye. I thought he would collapse into uncontrolled tears. My father did not respond.

Soon after Hora and Milka left Yael came with my daughters Katie and Eva. From the beginning my father responded more to the children than he had to anyone that day. They told him that they loved him and he replied that he loved them too. Blessed by an inspiration, Katie asked him whether he remembered a song he sang to her when she was little, sitting on his knee waiting for the dinner to cook. 'Oopa doopa, doopa, macaroni soupa.' She and Eva began to sing it, and to our amazement and joy he joined them, wanting even to go a second chorus. He then fell into silence, never to speak again.

Yael and the girls went to a motel while I stayed at the hospital. At ten o'clock nurses came to turn my father onto his other side. As they began to do it, he moaned in obvious pain. I pleaded with them to leave him be. They said that hospital regulations required them to turn him to prevent bed sores. I told them that he wouldn't live long enough for that, and pointed out the irony of the fact that the only time he showed pain was when they tried to ensure that he would not suffer it. Torn between the regulations and good sense, they allowed good sense to prevail.

I sat down to wait with him for his death. The nurses brought me a comfortable chair, one that would open into a bed, in case I slept the night. I reflected that just as I had been with him alone at Frogmore during the time of his terrible affliction, so I was now again alone with him in his mortal agony. And, as in my childhood, I spoke to him in German. I told him many times, '*Ich liebe dich, mein Vater.*' At first he opened his eyes each time I said it, but after a time he made no response.

My father died just past midnight, as they had predicted twenty-four hours before. I kissed him and sat with him for another half-hour before calling the nurses. I phoned Milka and told her that my father and her husband was dead. Then I went to my wife and my children who were waiting at the motel.

In the morning Yael, the girls and I went to Maryborough to be with Milka and also to arrange the funeral. As with Mitru and my mother, it was entrusted to Phelans, and as with Mitru and my mother, it was arranged that my father would lie in an open coffin for his mourners to see him for the last time. It was a

European custom and I knew that my father's relatives expected it, but remembering Mitru's funeral I forbade photographs.

I asked the funeral director whether the local paper, the *Maryborough Advertiser*, accepted obituaries. He phoned to check. The editor was out, apparently chasing a mountain lion which he believed to have killed cattle and sheep, tearing out their innards and leaving the carcass. I remembered the night my father and I sat behind a log in Carisbrook and could barely hold back my tears.

The funeral was on Monday, a day before my fiftieth birthday. I asked a friend, Peter Steele, who is also a priest, if he would conduct the service and bury my father. He agreed. Over the years he had heard me speak of my father, and on the night before the funeral we dined in Carlton and I told him, in summary, what I have written in this book. The next morning we drove through Maldon to Baringhup and on to where Frogmore had been, before it was burnt down some years before in a grass fire. The bluestone dairy was still standing, but only some bricks, the concrete walls of the verandah, and a few twisted sheets of iron testified to the fact that a house had once stood next to it. At St Augustine's Church, Peter gave a fine service, as I knew he would.

I had asked Hora if he wanted to say a few words,

but he felt unable to. There was no one else who could do it, so I gave the eulogy myself. I spoke of my father's life, his values, his friendship with Hora and marriage to Milka, but I said almost nothing about my mother, nothing about Mitru, or Lydia, and I referred only elliptically to his mental breakdown. I hoped that what I left out would not compromise the truth of what I said. I concluded with these words:

> We sometimes express our most severe judgment of other people by saying that we will never again speak to them. I never heard my father say that nor can I imagine him saying it. That, perhaps more than anything else, testifies to his unqualified sense of common humanity with everyone he met. His severe judgment often caused pain, but the simple honesty of its expression, together with his unhesitating acceptance of those whom he judged so severely, convinces me that he never intentionally caused suffering to anyone. He was truly a man who would rather suffer evil than do it.

When I came out of the church I saw an elderly man, standing apart, leaning on a walking stick, obviously an Australian, looking like an archetype of the men from my childhood whose character I remembered with admiration and fondness in my eulogy. I did not recognise him. When I went towards him I saw that his eyes were filled with tears. It was Neil Mikkelsen, the man who had been kind to my mother, and who had fallen from the haystack when my father worked for him. 'Every word you spoke was true,' he said. 'Your father saved my life.'

His presence and his words moved me. I thought again of Frogmore and my life there with my father. I remembered my mother laughing as she talked with Mikkelsen at the chicken-wire gate.

My father was buried in the Maryborough cemetery, close to my mother.

AFTER ROMULUS
Raimond Gaita

In *After Romulus*, Raimond Gaita revisits the world of his deeply loved memoir and his childhood in central Victoria.

He writes about Hora, who was an inspiration to him throughout his life, about the making of the acclaimed film starring Eric Bana, about ideas of truth, the limits of character, and the conflict between love and morality. And, most movingly, about his mother Christine and his longing for her.

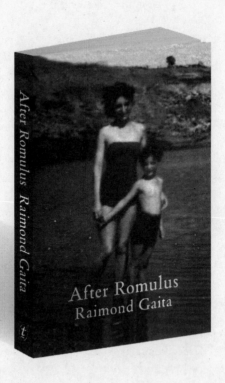

'[The essay] "An Unassuageable Longing" explains Christine and makes her real: she is finally chronicled with love and rigour, as was Romulus…In a book full of extraordinary revelations, this chapter will stay long in the reader's memory.' *Age*

'It is a towering piece, intimate and rational, a love song, an elegy…This is a moving book.' *Courier-Mail*

'It is impossible not to be moved by this achingly raw remembrance and grateful for the stunning candour of its author.' *Sunday Age*

'In *After Romulus* Raimond Gaita invites us into the far reaches of his considerable mind and the deep places of his soul. This will be felt as a privilege by most readers, as it should. And it is, as it turns out, not just a sequel, but an extension of all that was good in his initial story. It is a book to stretch the mind and enlarge the heart.' *Canberra Times*

'This is the kind of writing that is so brave it makes you flinch, so profound it makes you examine yourself, and so moving it makes you see life afresh. I was entranced as usual by Rai Gaita's limpid style, and his signature combination of philosophical intellect and warm heart.' Anna Funder

'This extraordinary book set me reflecting upon my own residency in the world—my own decency, condescension, loves and truths.' *Weekend Herald* (NZ)

'Gaita is a brave, decent and emotionally intelligent man…we need more like him.' *Australian*

THE PHILOSOPHER'S DOG
Raimond Gaita

What does Raimond Gaita's dog, Gypsy, think about when she sits on her mat gazing out to sea?
Is it mistaken to attribute the concepts of love, devotion, grief or friendship to animals? Why do we care so much for some creatures and so little for others? How do animals think and feel, and what is it that defines the relations between them and us? In this marvellous book Raimond Gaita tells stories about animals he has known and looks at the work of other writers, from J. M. Coetzee and Hannah Arendt to Ludwig Wittgenstein and René Descartes, to offer a different way of thinking about animals and about ourselves.

'That truly rare thing: an accessible book of philosophy undiminished in intellectual rigour.'
Age

'Clever and energetic…[Gaita's] ability to spin his philosophy from tales of everyday life is remarkable.' *Australian*

'Reads like a book of parables…*The Philosopher's Dog* is thoughtful, touching and utterly admirable.'
Big Issue

A COMMON HUMANITY:
THINKING ABOUT LOVE & TRUTH & JUSTICE
Raimond Gaita

'Raimond Gaita's insights are original and his prose
is as eloquent as it is affecting.'
Economist, Books of the Year, 2000

'This is a remarkable book…an original contribution to
moral philosophy utterly free from the technicalities of the
profession…Though profound and in places difficult, the book
demands of its reader only careful thought and an engagement
with the moral seriousness out of which it was written. Gaita's
book is an absorbing read from beginning to end.'
Tim Crane, University College London

'This philosophy for the educated public is
philosophy at its most profound.'
Australian Book Review

'A rare and distinguished contribution to our public life.'
Australian's Review of Books

'A wonderful piece of writing. The disciplined
individuality of Gaita's voice shows how a humanly
serious practice of philosophy might make a decisive
contribution to our public culture.'
Stephen Mulhall, New College, Oxford